IN
DEFENSE
OF WHOM?

IN DEFENSE OF WHOM?

A Critique of Criminal Justice Reform

Gregg Barak

D. Crim.
University of California/Berkeley

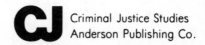

Criminal Justice Studies
Anderson Publishing Co.

Table of Contents

Introduction

An article in *Time* entitled "Crime: Why—and What to Do," states that "The whole system—from criminal code to prison release—must be reformed within a single perspective to speed, regularize, and rationalize the process of law enforcement. The choice . . . is whether we dispense justice or dispense with it."[1] This statement reflects a tragic omission in logic. The authors are assuming that once the present system of justice is made more efficient, the demands of justice will be met. Unfortunately, this assumption is invalid and dangerous. Justice is not possible in a society that denies social justice. Justice is not realized by merely punishing those who react against social inequality.

Studies of crime and criminal justice typically use the legal code as the starting point for their investigations and analyses: "crime" is behavior that violates the criminal law, "criminals" are persons who engage in such behavior, and "criminal justice" is the administration and enforcement of "neutral law." Consequently, reform movements have been and continue to be predominantly concerned with the reform and regulation of legally-defined and adjudicated "criminals." In keeping with these definitions of who needs to be controlled and how, the purposes of crime control as espoused by such academic disciplines as law, criminology, and criminal justice have repeatedly functioned as the intellectual strongarm of the State.[2]

Although social conditions have been squarely recognized as the primary cause of crime, most of our corrective efforts have been directed toward rehabilitating the criminal rather than toward revamping the socio-economic system. Most victims of social injustice who commit crimes are given attention only after the crimes are committed. Criminologists, sociologists, and psychologists are quick to examine a criminal's past to explain his deviant behavior, yet it is commonly demanded that the criminal and not society change radically.

To return to society, the criminal must be able—whether he is truly "rehabilitated" or not—to adjust to the inequities that were at the root of his crime. His ability to tolerate his position in society dictates his success as a "reformed" citizen. At the same time, instead of attempting to make fundamental changes in the social structure so crime would be substantially reduced, reformers try instead merely to modify the administration of criminal justice so it measures up to democratic concepts of law and order. In short, criminal justice reform, despite its "liberal" rhetoric, has been directed toward the reformation not of society but of its victims.

What distinguishes liberal reform from more fundamental criticisms is the belief that it is possible to create an orderly *and* humanitarian system of criminal justice within the context of existing economic and political arrangements. It is true that liberal criminologists, particularly in recent years, have subjected crime control institutions (police, prisons, courts) to a variety of criticisms, including inefficiency, mismanagement, corruption, and brutality, but their solutions to these problems are invariably formulated within the framework of the existing social order. Reform, in the liberal mind, means adjustment to, not fundamental changes of, the institutions that regulate the present social order. For example, Edwin Schur, in a popular textbook on criminology and social policy, calls for reforms that include alterations in the social structure, but he maintains that these reforms can be achieved "well within the bounds of a viable capitalism."[3] Obviously, liberal criminologists believe we can discuss criminality while at the same time ignoring for the most part the political and economic factors that produced that society.

Unfortunately, it has been more advantageous for order to condemn the common criminal and ignore the crimes committed by the elite members of society; in other words, to recognize that crimes, especially street crimes, are, in reality, rational and *not* irrational acts is not conducive to the maintenance of our criminal justice system. When crimes are recognized as rational responses to social or economic conditions, it is only reasonable to direct efforts toward changing those conditions rather than punishing anyone who reacts negatively to them. That is, how can punishment be justified for acts that are only reasonable given a person's social and economic situation?

One purpose of this study is to demonstrate the relationship between developing political and economic structures and juridical forms. By tracing the historical relationship between the development of our capitalistic system and the rise of liberal democratic thought in the nineteenth and twentieth centuries, analysts can discern two approaches to criminal justice reform.

First, there are reforms that emerge out of the exchange of power between the criminal justice system and the larger political order. These relationships are characteristic, Habermas states, of the "growing interdependençe of research, technology, and governmental administration, which has converted the system of sciences into a primary force of production."[4] Within the context of what Habermas is saying, the criminal justice system has geared itself toward satisfying governmental needs; research, rather than being "pure," is geared toward realizing the mutual goals of the criminal justice system and the political order.

Second, there are the self-deceiving attempts of liberal reformists. Their attempts at reform can be defined as "reformist reforms" rather than "structural reforms."[5] "Liberal reformism" can also be defined as "interventionist activity which is designed to secure the stability and growth of the economic system."[6] "Reformist reforms" are reforms that do not address the need for structural changes in the fundamental relationships in a capitalistic society; that formal legal equality and extreme social inequality exist side by side has been recognized but conveniently forgotten in the actual implementation of superficial reforms. Thus, the contradictions of a class society are given little more than lip service in most discussions on crime control and criminal justice social policy. In short, for the past seventy-five years, liberal reforms within the administration of criminal justice have been designed to rationalize a crime control apparatus that is a reflex of class-stratified society.

Reforms that ignore the ways in which the law is distorted to serve the needs of the capitalistic system cannot eliminate the inequitable character of justice that has existed in America since its beginning. The sociological view of law is inadequate because it does not take into account the various forces of the political economy that have created and shaped the interests and claims of the criminal law. Moreover, the criminal justice system, when taken as a whole, is not analyzed as an evolving set of legal relations interdependent with the parallel development of other social and political, and most importantly, economic institutions. On the contrary, the criminal justice system is mistakenly regarded as a static and self-contained bureaucracy. Because reformers do not recognize the impingement of the economic system upon the administration of the law, they are content to restrict their efforts to modest reorganization and gradual expansion, all within the framework of what they regard as a sound and enduring political economy.

The recent works of Isaac Balbus, Mark Kennedy, Alan Wolfe, the Schwendingers, Tony Platt, Richard Quinney, Barry Krisberg, and Taylor, Walton, and Young contend that the conventional analyses of crime and crime control only serve to maintain the social relations of capitalistic society.[7] They argue that crime control is the socio-political expression of the dialectics of bourgeois legality—a set of legal relationships that have been evolving since the early emergence of capitalism. Thus, the level of analysis moves away from the discussions of rule of the law and due process as these relate to the ideals of the United States Constitution and toward the more concrete realities of societal law enforcement as related to the political economy of capitalism. These realities have brought forth a New Criminology.

A primary purpose of this study is to re-examine the criminal justice system and to help clarify and expand the developing ideas of the New Criminology. Attempts are made to explain legal reform movements in twentieth-century America by analyzing the emergence of the public defender system. Focus shifts from a general analysis of liberal reformism and ideology to the more specific political, economic, and social forces that brought changes in crime control strategies during the Progressive Era.

In keeping with the New Criminology, this book argues that the traditional accounts of both the creation and the function of the public defender in the administration of criminal justice are not only an oversimplification, but a misinterpretation of history.

Instead of viewing the public defender as the product of admiration for due process and the ideals of justice, it can be argued that the emergence of the public defender resulted from a changing political economy. In short, during the transition from a society based on a laissez-faire economy to one based on monopoly capitalism, the public defender as "social policy" appeared as an accommodating reform in criminal justice administration.

The underlying theme of this book is that it is insufficient to study the administration of criminal justice from the perspective of the idealized concepts of law (constitutional due process) or from the perspective of the social realities of its application (bureaucratic due process), or from the combined perspective of the two. For while these concepts of criminal justice provide some standards for analysis, neither is sufficient to make evident the relationships between the needs of the criminal justice system and the needs of the larger political order. This work is not a definitive history of the public defender but rather a study of the criminal justice system in a socio-economic context. History is used as a tool for understanding the critical relationships involved in political jurisprudence.

NOTES

1. "Crime: Why—And What to Do." *Time,* May 18, 1975, p. 18.
2. Tony Platt, "Prospects for a Radical Criminology in the United States," *Crime and Social Justice,* Spring-Summer Issue, 1974, p. 1.
3. Edwin Schur, *Our Criminal Society* (Englewood Cliffs: Prentice-Hall, 1969), p. 190.
4. Jurgen Habermas, *Theory and Practice* (Boston: Beacon Press, 1974), p. 5.
5. Andre Gorz, *Strategy for Labor: A Radical Proposal* (Boston: Beacon Press, 1964), p. 33.
6. Habermas, *Theory and Practice,* p. 4.
7. Richard Quinney, *Class, State, and Crime: On the Theory and Practice of Criminal Justice* (New York: McKay Co., Inc., 1977), p. v.

1 CRIMINAL LAW / CRIMINAL JUSTICE: The Foundation

The decline of mercantilism and the rise of laissez-faire capitalism in nineteenth century America influenced the relationship between government and legal institutions. The right to acquire and protect property became a predominant issue in the development of a democratic society. The prevailing emphasis on the importance of private property had a subsequent effect on the development of criminal law. Concomitantly, the formation of the criminal justice system reflected the current romantic preoccupation with individual rights and freedom. The rural and agrarian culture, the respect for individualism, and the expansionist outlook of both industrial entrepreneurs and frontier farmers influenced the development of a decentralized and independent criminal justice system in pioneer America.

Criminal Law and Private Property

John Hancock, as early as 1793, defined the functions of the criminal law in the spirit of laissez-faire. First, the criminal law was to punish and deter direct attacks on private property, and second, the criminal law was to preserve the order and power of government so that the first function could be fulfilled.[1]

Prior to the Jacksonian administrations, Senator Thomas Hart Benton of Missouri, a businessman and constitutional lawyer, listed three important responsibilities of the State under a laissez-faire system of government:

(1) It had to maintain the basic framework of the system (such as that of money and the rule of law); (2) it had to preserve the com-

1

petitive situation by acting against monopolies and by helping new or weak entrants into the scramble; and (3) it had to be the agent in expanding and protecting the marketplace, which was the key to individual competition producing the general welfare.[2]

During the Jacksonian period, laissez-faire capitalism and individualism were buttressed by a "hands-off" governmental policy. Amos Kendall, a member of Jackson's Kitchen Cabinet, explained to Congress that "things will take their course in the moral as well as the natural world" as long as Congressmen were not only "content to let currency and private business alone," but also to leave common "individuals and states as much as possible to themselves."[3]

At the same time, however, Jacksonian democracy was waging a struggle against privilege and aristocracy in an effort to reduce special favors accorded early capitalists. The anti-elitist and anti-professional sentiment of the times was a reaction, in part, to the conservative rule under the Federalists who were accused of conspiring to overthrow the purposes of the American Revolution. Specifically, complaints were leveled at the access to power, prosperity, and influence in a political rather than a social or economic sense. Rush Welter in *The Mind of America* (1820–1860) writes:

> In Jacksonian eyes, an 'aristocrat' was someone who was empowered by law to affect the economic and social welfare of his contemporaries, or who enjoyed legal privileges that he could turn to his own account in an otherwise competitive economy. Democrats discerned 'aristocracy' in a wide range of traditional republican measures through which the states and the national government had sought to foster public services like banking, transportation and education by offering wealthy men the means and motives to place their resources where the state judged they would do the most good. The sole result, so far as the Jacksonians were concerned, was a social order in which some men benefited from the labor of others—an order in which, according to the classic Democratic argument, prejudicial laws allowed some men to extract wealth from the pockets of other men by legal rather than economic means.[4]

Throughout the middle period of American history, monopolies and corporations were viewed as intrinsically evil because they rested upon privileges not granted to everyone.

For instance, during the 1843 gubernatorial campaign in Missouri, John C. Edwards, recognizing the privilege of limited liability of stockholders for the debts of their corporations, advocated

> repealing all laws which exempt or relieve members of corporations from individual responsibility, and of passing a general law making members of corporations individually responsible for the acts of the corporation. All men should be held responsible for their just debts, no matter in what capacity they may be contracted.[5]

Edwards' concept of democracy is reflected in the assertion that "all men should be held responsible for their just debts."

The concepts of "equal rights" and "equal responsibility" ("all men should be held responsible for their just debts") supported the democratic notion of the "general good." The "general good" did not refer to the promotion of riches and power, but to the

> Equal protection of every citizen in his rights—the impartial administration of justice, the supremacy of the laws, in their power of punishment and protection, over all—equal means of wealth, education, and advancement to every citizen—the universal diffusion of intelligence and the promotion of honesty, industry, and virtue among every class,—and the subordination of all mere pecuniary and temporary interests to the good of man, in all his moral and immoral qualities.[6]

Economic policies that hinted of privilege and did not support the goal of establishing "equal means of wealth" for all citizens were severely criticized. The tariff, eminent domain, the joint privilege of transportation and manufacturing, and the banking privileges associated with canal, turnpike, and manufacturing enterprises became national issues (i.e., issues that revolved around the fear of privilege as opposed to the protection of the general good). The national sentiment of the times was that the general good was assured as long as every citizen was afforded the equal opportunity to acquire wealth; that as long as this opportunity was open to all peoples, isolated power and privilege could not threaten the democratic order.

Democratic idealism, as reflected in this national trust in man's inherent goodness, promoted superficial ideas of what constituted "unAmerican" activities. The American public, in other words, could not foresee the consequences of the prevailing notion that freedom was best realized in the opportunity for everyone to acquire property. Consider Levi Slamm's endorsement of "virtuous" wealth:

> I am no enemy to wealth when honestly acquired, either by mental or physical exertion, or even inherited from those who have so acquired it, it is no more a crime than virtuous poverty. . . . I would remove every obstacle in the road to wealth, every act of legislation conferring advantages to the *few,* and adding unjustly to the burdens of the *many,* and confine legislation to its purely legitimate object, *protection to person and property.*[7]

An inequitable social system emerged as a consequence of an initial trust in a collective democratic conscience. By the turn of the century, industrialism and the accumulation of wealth, unimpeded by laissez-faire, developed into a corporate hegemony over the American society. Despite the number of egalitarian reforms (e.g., stay and exemption laws, mechanic's lien laws, impetus for abolishing feudal tenures), efforts to achieve an egalitarian order failed because of an inability to understand and neutralize the power of private property.

Criminal Justice and Individual Rights

The early formation of criminal law and the criminal justice system in the United States developed as a reaction against the harsh and brutal practices of the Tudors and the Stuarts. In England, the criminal laws were overzealous to say the least:

> Cutting down a young tree, impersonating a pensioner, stealing linen left out to bleach, defacing a county bridge, and two hundred and nineteen other offenses were punishable by death until 1837.[8]

The laws of criminal procedure were stringent too:

> Indictments were drawn in a language which the accused could not read, and frequently he did not know with what crime he was

charged until the day of his trial. He was not allowed to testify in his own behalf. His witnesses were allowed to be sworn but their evidence naturally had but little weight. If accused of treason or felony, his counsel could not even address the jury. When, in spite of such tremendous odds, an accused man had enough ability and natural eloquence to combat successfully the able lawyers for the crown, and persuade a jury to acquit him, the members of this jury might be fined and imprisoned.[9]

And the actual punishments for crimes were bloody and barbarous:

In cases of treason, the convicted man was partially hanged, cut down and disemboweled and while still alive his entrails were burned before his eyes. Women guilty of the murder of their husbands were burned at the stake. Coiners were boiled alive. Suicides were buried at crossroads with a great stake driven through the heart.[10]

In England, from the late fifteenth century to the early seventeenth century, the protection of the individual from arbitrary, primitive justice was limited, and the rights of the accused were restricted. For example, there were no means by which the accused could determine the evidence to be used against him, nor could he, as a matter of right, secure a counselor or solicitor for advice as to his defense; he was not even allowed to speak with any of his witnesses.[11]

By the late seventeenth century, however, the idea of "equal rights" gained some footing in both the legislature and judiciary. The judicial order changed significantly, responding to the various scandals, especially the political trials (e.g., the Popish Plot, the Meal Tub Plot, the Rye House Plot, and the Seven Bishops) that were associated with the Duke of Monmouth's rebellion in the period between the Restoration in 1678 and the Revolution in 1688.

Legislative changes included: limitations on the power of judges; the requirement of good behavior rather than the pleasure of the Crown in order to hold office as a judge; extensions of the functions and powers of the jury; the swearing in of the defense witnesses; the use of counsel as an advocate; and a copy of the indictment for the defendant.[12]

Futhermore, judges began to set precedents and establish principles to counter the severity of the statutes. Judges also began to observe details and technicalities that would help limit discretionary decision making.

This trend in Anglo-Saxon law of limiting possible juridical abuse was also reflected in American policies regarding individual rights and the role of law in a developing nation. Generally, weak and decentralized government allowed farmers and merchants the freedom to expand their particular domains in a free market economy and to compete and acquire both property and capital with little legal interference.[13]

Government officials who were responsive to the needs of local communities were elected to office. Their terms of office were intentionally short; and if a judge failed to express the will of the people or tried a person without cause, a change in office would result.[14] Meanwhile, while the judge's powers were restricted, the powers of the jury and of lawyers were expanded. Concomitantly, the rights of the accused were extended (as in England) while the rights of the State were limited. In general, however, individual competition and Jacksonian romanticism supported the benefits of unrestrained liberty and the preference for private judgment of the law.

Roscoe Pound wrote in 1930 about the conflict between the traditional precepts of the law and the demands of a social reality based on new kinds of political and economic arrangements:

> Like the pioneer, too, the leader of industry was independent, self-reliant, versatile, inclined to business innovations demanding legal changes, and given to short cuts to desired results. Laws seemed to him, as the pioneer, at best a necessary evil. He felt that if a rule of law interfered with a business project, or even with some detail of one, there was not time for formal repeal or formal amendment. A way round must be found, by resort to the constitution, by interpretation, or if necessary by specious evasion.[15]

After describing various nineteenth century violations of the law, Pound explained that the infringements of law by good citizens ... the violent assertions of private judgment against statutes, the mob enforcements of the ethical customs of the locality, for the most part had behind them conscientious belief in a body of law of higher authority of which each individual's reason was the repository.[16]

A situation existed in which the laissez-faire spirited Americans believed that there was no point in the government doing what they could do equally well, or better, for themselves:

It was entirely possible for men who respected law and believed in order, believing also in natural rights and in sovereignty of the people, to conceive that offhand popular action, in accordance with their reasons and their consciences, dictated what was lawful in all but form.[17]

The role of government and the criminal law was not particularly to regulate individual behavior, but to preserve a socio-economic system that was conducive to the acquisition of private property.

A "Government of Men"

The English judicial system provided the foundation for the early colonial governments; the laws and appellate tribunals were modeled after English Privy Council. The colonial governors and their councils usually exercised authority over all branches of government—legislative, executive, and judicial. Colonial America did not distinguish between the three branches of government: general appellate jurisdiction was granted to a governor or one of his representatives. Before the end of the seventeenth century, however, Massachusetts had created a Superior Court exercising both appellate and original jurisdiction, with the right of direct appeal to the King in Council. These practices eventually became institutionalized in Pennsylvania, Rhode Island, Connecticut, Virginia, and New Hampshire. By the time of the American Revolution, there were two kinds of appellate courts—one made up of legislators (similar to the House of Lords) and the other of judges (similar to the King's Bench).

The judges of the trial courts, typically appointed by governors, carried out both trial and administrative functions. For example, "it was not unusual to find a judge whose duties included assessing and levying taxes, licensing trades, and appointing petty judicial officers."[18] After the war, the new Republic imposed a system of checks and balances that resulted in the separation of judicial from legislative and executive bodies.

Independence, self-reliance, versatility, impatience with the pompous and ceremonial, and a distrust of specialists and experts characterized the administration of a criminal justice system managed "by lay magistrates, by soldiers, clergymen, or administrative officers, and by legislative assemblies."[19] The laissez-faire attitudes of natural rights, democratic ideals, and expansionism contributed to the creation of an informal justice system that depended on the active participation of laymen who were supposedly equal to or better than the professionally trained person. Each male citizen was a personal judge of the law according to a philosophy that was consistent with and supportive of an independent political and legal order. The common citizen was in a position to "judge for himself, at the crises of action whether and how far to obey or enforce the law as it stands in the books,"[20] and to "judge of the law not merely to ascertain what it is, but to judge of its conformity to his personal ideals and to ascertain its validity."[21]

The "government of men" was dictated not only by the romantic mood of the times, but also by the agrarian nature of society. As late as 1840, ninety percent of the American population lived in rural communities. These communities were largely populated by a homogeneous citizenry, a situation which was conducive to developing a community consensus and a commonly shared understanding of local governmental institutions. Thus, the problems of criminal justice management and crime control were straight-forward. The criminal code was small and the number of offenders was minimal. The typical criminal, according to

Pound, was usually a neighbor who had temporarily "gone wrong" and committed an offense.

Despite the active local support and participation of citizens in the political and administrative decisions of government, the practice of extra-legal or "eye for an eye" justice was a common practice in the nineteenth century:

> Men were prone to set right their own wrongs, conduct feuds, organize vigilance committees, hold lynchings, and exert off-hand, extra-legal pressure on those whose conduct varied from the locally recognized ethical norm.[22]

The Court System

Laissez-faire justice adapted itself well to rural society. Because of rudimentary means of communication and expensive travel between communities, a court system of separate and independent jurisdictions responding to local needs emerged. As new towns sprung up and communities grew, more courts were established. Meanwhile, the conditions of life and crime gradually became more complex, and the technicalities within criminal procedure increased. The result was an accusational system that had blossomed within the spirit of individualism and competition.

On a community basis, trials and small criminal dockets proceeded at a pace that was gauged to meet the small volume of local business. Judges, juries, and lawyers all shared intimate and personal knowledge of events in the community. The will of the sovereign people prevailed as they participated in the administration of criminal law. And justice, more or less, was secured to the common satisfaction of the community.

Structurally, a formal, nationwide system of criminal justice did not exist in nineteenth-century America. There was a lack of organization and centralized responsibility. The courts were not unified and the jurisdictions overlapped. For instance, criminal courts were divided into a disjointed system of lower and upper courts. As late as 1920, Edwin Sutherland wrote:

> A city may have twenty justices of the peace, but they customarily act without reference to each other or to other courts. . . . In the courts in general there is no coordination of work; they are not organized.[23]

In the smaller communities, the lower courts consisted of justices of the peace, and in the large cities, such as New York and Chicago, they consisted of police courts, magistrate courts, and municipal courts. The lower courts handled petty cases, misdemeanors, and the preliminary hearings for felonies. All these early courts had limited jurisdictions. For example, the preliminary hearing, the grand jury indictment, and the trial would each take place in three separate courts. With respect to both the number of cases settled and the number of people affected, the lower courts dominated the upper courts.

The upper or superior courts consisted of county, district, and circuit courts. These courts were always open in the few large cities, but in most of rural America, sessions were held from four to eight times each year. Upper courts heard cases on appeal from the lower courts and had original jurisdiction over felonies. Toward the end of the nineteenth century, appellate courts and state supreme courts as we know them today appeared.

The time between arrest and final disposition was, on the average, two months. The type and nature of the indictments or accusations required the use of a grand jury rather than an information filed by the prosecutor. Indictments, adhering to tradition, were cumbersome and complex, demanding finical and verbose dispositions. Furthermore, any error in an indictment, whether relevant or not to the actual facts of the case, was grounds for a case being reversed. Cases were commonly reversed for a mistake in spelling or for an omitted word. In addition, attorneys for the defense could make numerous formal motions, thus causing innumerable delays. Sutherland comments on the common practices used by lawyers in trials conducted as late as 1910:

> It is not at all unusual for as many as fifteen formal motions to be

introduced in one case, each one involving debate, probable continuances, and decisions by the court. After the trial starts, the lawyer for the defense may secure one delay after another, by such motions as demurrer to the indictment, motion to inspect the minutes of the grand jury, motion to dismiss the indictment for lack of evidence, motion for a change of venue, motion for a commission to take testimony in the case.[24]

Judges during this period were increasingly suspect. Their growing subservience to political bosses and organized groups undermined public trust in judicial neutrality. Consequently, trial by jury rather than by judge came to be regarded as a necessary means of protecting the common people from corrupt judges.

The jury was cherished as a fundamental symbol of democracy, dating as far back as the Magna Carta (1215) and was an important force in the criminal court throughout the nineteenth century. The procedural tasks of the jury were two: first, the jury (grand jury) functioned as the accusatorial agent providing information on community affairs and, more importantly, deciding whether or not the facts of a case warranted an indictment; second, the jury functioned to determine the guilt or innocence of the accused person. With respect to the dual role played by a "jury of one's peers," the state criminal courts depended on the active participation of community members. During this period, the jury system came to be viewed as the bulwark of liberty, the guardian of individual rights.

The Deterioration of Laissez-Faire Criminal Justice (1880–1930)

The prevailing concept of law and order in pioneer-America—"an eye for an eye"—was appropriate as long as crimes were simple, their resolution obvious. It was recognized, nevertheless, that in certain cases only the court could serve as an effective intermediary in the resolution of legal conflicts. With the added assurance that legal technicalities were adhered to, thus protecting the people from the whims of corrupted judges, Anglo-Saxon trends in protecting individual rights and the laissez-faire spirit of individual justice worked hand in hand. The gradual deteration of laissez-faire criminal justice is discussed in the following sections of this chapter.

Transformation of American Society: Emerging Conflict

The growing population, the increasing number of immigrants from southern and eastern Europe, rapid communication and transportation, the appearance of a wage-earning class, and the widening conflicts of interest in a newly heterogeneous society, all contributed to the demise of laissez-faire criminal justice. The system of law enforcement and control, designed for a homogeneous, pioneer, and primarily agricultural society, was ill-adapted to the needs of an increasingly complex, urban, and industrialized society. Nathanial F. Cantor, a sociologist of crime and criminal justice, writes:

> The ease of movement . . . prevents the easy stabilization of community life. Traditions of social responsibility and community welfare cannot thrive in a heterogeneously populated country characterized by many conflictive cultural patterns.[25]

The criminal justice system of a simpler agrarian economy was not equipped to deal with increasing class and racial antagonisms brought on by the enormous changes in the social organization and by various technological developments during the post-Civil War period:

> America was rapidly moving toward industrialism. City streets were crowded, for immigrants were arriving in great numbers. The criminal justice system was hard pressed to meet the challenge. Police forces were organized along [Sir Robert] Peel's lines. Officers for the first time wore distinguished blue uniforms, which were inspired by the clothing of the Union Soldiers.

> This period saw a fundamental change in American values. The country was being transformed from an agricultural nation to a heavily industrialized, urban society. In this society immigrant groups became powerful political forces. State governments, how-

ever, continued to be dominated by rural legislators. The laws which were passed often reflected agrarian, Anglo-Saxon Protestant values. Since many cities had Irish Catholic and immigrant leadership, conflict was inevitable. Many state laws were under-enforced or altogether ignored in urban areas.[26]

Overcrowded conditions within the criminal justice system were becoming a serious problem. The U.S. prison population, for example, between 1870–1904, rose nearly sixty-two percent; and between 1904–1935, it rose one-hundred and forty percent.[27] The responses to the rising number of accused and convicted criminals included the institutionalization of the plea bargaining system and the building of state penitentiaries. Sixteen states found it necessary between 1870–1900 to construct prisons, some of the more famous being Yuma in Arizona (1875), Folsom in California (1880), and Walla Walla in Washington (1886).[28]

As the number of defendants continued to rise, accomodations had to be made. In order to alleviate courthouse congestion, the agents of adjudication began to reduce or drop some of the charges against the accused as incentive to plead guilty so that trials, especially time-consuming jury trials, could be avoided. Consequently, throughout this period, there was a steady increase in the number of dropped and reduced charges; this was evidenced by the increased number of proportional convictions after pleas of guilty as compared with convictions by juries, particularly in large cities such as New York and Chicago.[29]

By the turn of the century, the initial laissez-faire emphasis on the right to acquire private property blossomed into a full-fledged national preoccupation with wealth and power. Political corruption became widespread and political machines dominated urban areas:

> The [political] machines controlled the city governments, including the police and the courts. Payrolls were padded and payoffs were collected from contractors. The citizens didn't mind though. "Padded payrolls were better than no payrolls," they said.[30]

But graft was not only "white graft" (from contractors) but

also "dirty graft" (from lawbreakers). Both forms of bribery contributed to a changing national morality. "Rackets," "pull," and "protection" were common antidotes for stubborn legal nuisances. Prevailing values of wealth and success predominated as guiding principles of right and wrong. Cantor states:

> The ability to 'make good' and 'get away with it' offsets the questionable means employed in the business as well as professional world. Disrespect for the law and order is the accompanying product of this scheme of success.[31]

Cantor also speaks explicitly of a social system where one either exploits or is exploited:

> Of more fundamental importance is the accelerated expansion of our industrial and commercial life. One outstanding effect of the new economic order has been the development of new types of business organization which have become interdependent. Big business has succeeded in utilizing the nineteenth century legal and political machinery for shaping governmental policies. With such control, they can secure their interests while the people at large are exploited. The exploited, in turn, with this pattern before them, seek to become exploiters.[32]

Using softer language, and perhaps somewhat apologetically, President Taft in 1905 said:

> Some of the causes for the lax administration of the criminal law may be found in the lenient, happy-go-lucky character of the American people, absorbed in their own affairs, not fully realizing that this tremendous evil exists in the community.[33]

The Demise of Individual Justice

The informal mechanisms of social control that functioned in the nineteenth century could not continue in the twentieth. The National Economic League's Committee for "Efficiency in the Administration of Justice" reported in 1916 that "the informal agents of social control have withered away."[34] No longer did the household, neighborhood opinion, or religious commitment restrain individual behavior. Furthermore, the growth of formal agencies (e.g., police, probation, and social work) and the expanding state apparatus usurped the older informal institutions of crime control such as blood feuds and ostracism. And finally, the changing economic order was undermining former political, legal, and administrative relationships of rural communities.

With the breakdown of the common-law policy, the individual lost his initiative in the enforcement of law and order. Cantor writes about the loss of interest in local politics resulting from the growing corporate economic structure and its control of communities "from the outside":

> Indifference toward local politics, which has much to do with the administration of justice, results when economic interests are no longer governed by the laws operating in one's place of residence. With a shifting population, a huge labor turnover, and rapid and easy transportation, sustained and intelligent participation in politics and legislation is unlikely.[35]

The Abuse of Procedural Safeguards

As individual involvement in law enforcement dwindled, the emphasis on legal protection of individual rights lost its impetus. Those procedural safeguards inherited from England to counteract arbitrary and unfair application of the law were losing their places in the changing social and legal order of America. The growing abuse of three specific legal customs—the strict observation of legalistic details and technicalities, the tenet of "presumption of innocence" in law, and the role of the grand jury—contributed significantly to the decay of the criminal justice system of the laissez-faire era.

Legalism

The American criminal procedure that developed during the nineteenth century in reaction to the severity of the procedural rules of seventeenth and eighteenth century England was too inefficient and expensive for a growing industrial nation. Both legal scholars and legal reformers were critical of the existing practices of criminal justice: various rules within criminal procedure were held responsible for the intricate and time-consuming steps involved in criminal prosecutions. Criminal procedure was criticized for being too full of technicalities, demurrers, and safeguards. The results were cumbersome trials, a back-log of cases, and rising costs in the operation of criminal courts.

Legal technicalities were denounced as anachronistic and contrary to the needs of a growing society. They were seen as contributing to a vague and tedious administration of the law:

> We have unnecessarily fettered ourselves, have furnished a multitude of technical avenues of escape to wrong-doers, and have created a popular contempt for courts of justice, which shows itself in the sentimental and careless verdicts of juries, in a lack of public spirit, and in an indisposition to prosecute wrong-doers.[36]

Rules demanding absolute precision and accuracy were also blamed for the tremendous number of acquittals and mistrials:

> An error in complaint, a failure to arraign the prisoner, the admission of improper evidence, improper remarks by judges or counsel, erroneous instructions to the jury [can result in a dismissal of the case].[37]

Besides delaying legal proceedings, legal technicalities became playthings in the hand of calculating lawyers. Trials became a game of wits between contentious lawyers. Contested litigations not only delayed the criminal process, but fostered the game of "beat the law" among lawyers:

> It is frequently charged that the machinery of the law can be so manipulated that by means of wearing and dilatory tactics and expensive processes, a litigant with no justice in his cause but possessed of riches can effectually deprive a poor suitor of his rights and [in criminal trials] defeat a prosecutor. As time passes on, sentiment dies, and witnesses disappear, and a large number of this Bar [San Francisco] stand ready, for a fee, to pander to the man property in this prostitution of the law.[38]

This fraudulent legalism led to a disrespect for the law and the criminal justice system in general:

A belief that the course of criminal justice is slow and uncertain, that the chances are all in favor of the defendant, and that he has but to resort to technicalities to secure not only indefinite delay but ultimate freedom, breeds an indifference amounting almost to arrogance among lawbreakers, powerful and otherwise.[39]

What emerged in the last quarter of the century was a "lavish granting of new trials," resulting "in about twenty-nine percent of the cases received in the state courts" being tried again.[40] Harold A. Lehman, author of "A Critical Survey of Certain Phases of Trial Procedure in Criminal Cases," wrote that the common postponements of the criminal trials for counsel's unpreparedness, the absenteeism of witnesses, the nonpresence of material evidence, and the other legal manipulations used by lawyers and sanctioned by statutes or decisions could no longer be justified in the context of a growing industrial nation.

Exacerbating the growing misuse of legalism was the decentralization of the courts. As the population grew, the number of tribunals multiplied. Each court was characterized by a fixed staff and by a well-defined jurisdiction. Pound writes about the administration of justice at the turn of the century:

In the purely administrative phases of criminal justice, our uncentralized and non-cooperative regime of independent local jurisdictions and of independent authorities working each in its own way in the same locality is an anachronism in the economically unified land of today.[41]

Not only did the decentralization of courts impede an efficient administration of justice, because preliminary hearings, indictments, and trials were heard by separate courts, "piecemeal justice" prevailed. This situation was condemned as wasteful and expensive, specifically because the common elements of a case had to be repeated in its entirety to each tribunal. Consequently, the administration of justice was seen as being unnecessarily complicated and time-consuming.

Presumption of Innocence

A major tenet in courtroom philosophy since the early thirteenth century was that presumption of innocence is a necessary starting point in an equitable application of law and justice; that because of the extreme nature of punishment (as practiced in England), the burden of proof must lie with the prosecution. At the time, however, when legal protection from tyrants was no longer applicable, it was argued that the presumption of innocence, among other procedural safeguards, was no longer reasonable:

> The present overgrown state of the criminal law is the direct result of our exaggerated regard for personal liberty, coupled with a wholesale adoption of the technicalities of English law invented when only such technicalities could stand between the minor offender and the barbarous punishments of a bygone age.[42]

According to Samuel Scoville, a lawyer belonging to the bars of both New York City and Boston, the burden of proof properly belonged with the defense; the defense, in other words, was required to overcome the presumption of guilt which is naturally attached to the accusation. Scoville argues that a presumption of innocence was protecting the guilty and *not* the innocent:

> Today, in addition to this presumption of innocence which is protection enough, we are still conducting our criminal courts under out-worn technicalities which were devised to save innocent men but which are now used only to shield guilty ones and which have been abolished in England, the country where they originated, for over thirty years.[43]

The Grand Jury System of Indictment

The grand jury system of indictment had also out-lived its purposes. Its role, to protect the accused against overzealous prosecution, was no longer necessary. Cantor writes:

> The protection against oppressive prosecution afforded the accused is no longer required. Under our present court system, the possible abuses of legal authority and judicial discretion are subject to various appeals and reviews. The rights of the individual are carefully safeguarded without a grand jury indictment.[44]

The grand jury was attacked for being burdensome, redundant, and outdated in the early twentieth century. For
example, the work conducted by the grand jury (e.g., investigation of the alleged crime, accusing or indicting the defendant) was also being performed by the prosecution and
the police. Cantor, in an analysis of the breakdown of and
dissatisfaction with the administration of justice writes,
"This duplication of effort is wasteful and, when the several
groups do not wish or fail to co-operate, often aggravates
their inefficiency."[45]

The Sale of Justice

There existed a popularly shared dissatisfaction not only
with the administration of criminal justice, but with the
people assigned to operate and enforce the criminal law. In
1926 one critic wrote,

> One of the most pitiful spectacles in our municipal life is that of a
> horde of offenders, which we have been at great pains and expense
> to detect and arrest, passing through the meshes of our police
> courts which venal machine politicians with their army of "fixers"
> have been at equal pain to make large enough to provide easy
> egress.[46]

The committee on Legal Ethics of the San Francisco Bar
Association asserted to the President and Members in 1910
that:

> There is a growing lack of confidence in the impartiality and integ-
> rity of the judiciary. The belief is current that lawyers and inter-
> ests deemed to have been instrumental in securing the nomination
> and election to office of diverse members of the judiciary are pecul-
> iarly potent in matters coming before the bench, and that our
> judges are trammelled by political obligations and aspirations in
> the performance of their duties. Complaint is very general that our
> courts base their decisions rather on hair-splitting technicalities
> than upon the real merits of the cases. It is commonly charged
> against some of our judges that they perform little work, shirk
> trials, read little law, and are neither sufficiently educated nor
> experienced in the law to have justified their advancement to the
> offices they held.[47]

The scandals and corruption known to spring from a highly politicized courtroom were contributing to the popular "sale of justice" attitude in America:

> The problems of law enforcement today cannot be met with the decentralized agencies of the nineteenth century. The inability to fix responsibility and the inability of the police, prosecuting attorney and courts to act independently permits politics to enter at every step in the administration of justice, especially since the election or appointment to administrative office depends upon the political support.[48]

Public knowledge of "fixed" cases, corrupt judges, crooked bail bondsmen, "shysters," dishonest and economically motivated corporate lawyers, and political influences in the judicial process caused a general disrespect for law and order. According to Cantor, corruption existed in almost every major metropolitan area in the country, including Philadelphia, Chicago, Cleveland, Kansas City, Los Angeles, San Francisco, and New York City. Kenneth Johnson, in a recent book, *The Bar Association of San Francisco: The First Hundred Years,* writes:

> In the early part of the century the position of the bench and the bar in public opinion was not high. Lawyers were considered tricky and motivated largely by a desire for fees. The public also had some doubts about its judges. Many believed that decisions were determined by political consideration, friendships, and behind-the-scenes payments. Even attorneys were saying that "it is better to know the judge than the law.[49]

Johnson, in his account of the San Francisco Bar, describes in some detail the famous Boss Ruef Scandal of 1906 and the associated political trials. The scandal involved Mayor E. Schartz, over fifty prominent lawyers, and of course, Abraham Ruef, an attorney described then as having "an excellent mind, great political ambition, and boundless avarice."[50] The incident involved graft among such corporations as United Railroad Company, Parkside Realty Company, and The French Restaurants. Johnson, concluding his discussion of the scandal, notes that "it is of interest that out of all the indictments and trials only one defendant reached the penitentiary, Abraham Ruef."[51]

Trial judges were not exempt from contributing to national dissatisfaction with the administration of criminal justice. Criticism was aimed at both the office itself and the judges in office. It was generally felt that the office was controlled by politicians. The functional obligations of the office were said to handcuff trial judges, prohibiting them from sufficiently directing the trial process. For example, judges were prevented from commenting on evidence or the refusal of a defendant to take the stand. The role of umpire was considered too weak a position for the judge to play. William E. Mikell, Dean of the Law School of the University of Pennsylvania in the twenties, notes that:

> In many of our states the legislative changes in criminal procedure represent the desires of lawyers for the defense who wish to reduce the judge, when an issue of fact is submitted to the jury, to the position of a police officer at a prize fight, the contestants being the lawyers.[52]

And the Committee on Efficiency in the Administration of Justice maintains that:

> The unfortunate situation in which the judge sits as a mere umpire in a game between counsel grew up under an elective bench and is to be found chiefly, if not wholly, where the judiciary is elected for short terms. Lack of control over the bar on the part of judges, who cannot insist upon expedition without imperiling their positions, is not the least cause of unnecessary continuances and postponements and of the wranglings of counsel and the unfortunate treatment of witnesses which have cast discredit upon American trials.[53]

Judicial credibility was also being undermined by subjective applications of the law. Pound states: "Even judges have been known to warp the law in order to prevent convictions where they were not in sympathy with oversevere laws or extreme penalties."[54] Although judges occupied a relatively weak position in the courtroom, the fact that they could interpret the law was regarded suspiciously. Sentence disparities confessed to an unwonted power that was not only unwarranted but dangerous.

In comparison to the relatively impotent position of the judge, the jury was considered to possess far too much power. Their influence was felt throughout the criminal justice system. Pound writes:

> Juries prove unwilling to subject the concrete offender to the severe penalties which the zeal of the lawmaker lays down for the abstract offender. It has happened also that pressure upon lawmakers has led them to impose penalties upon acts for which juries will not agree to subject men to punishment . . .[55]

Although the jury was now thought to be without the knowledge or competence necessary to evaluate the facts of law, it retained the same amount of power which was afforded it during the nineteenth century. Pound writes about the imbalance of power between the judge and the jury:

> The judge is made quite powerless to control the trial, and the jury becomes an independent tribunal with a large scope for disregarding or nullifying the law.[56]

The jury system was also attacked for being too costly in both time and money. Another common criticism of the jury was the requirement of unanimous decision for a conviction. One of the better descriptions of the jury system is contained in this address to the president and members of the Bar Association of San Francisco:

> The jury system has acquired the disrespect and the distrust of a very large body of our citizens. There is a belief in many quarters that large interests, corporate and other, maintain bureaus whose business it is to improperly influence jurors, or upon special occasions agencies are invoked for the same corrupt purpose. The feeling is often heard expressed that justice cannot be had from juries in civil causes, notably in damage suits for personal injuries against public service corporations. It is charged that sometimes corrupt juries are deliberately selected; that at other times jurors are corrupted during the trial, and that the admonitions of the courts to jurors not to discuss with third persons or among themselves the cause on trial, are generally and habitually disregarded.[57]

Finally, all lawyers, especially in the practice of criminal law, were severely criticized. The legal profession was disorganized and without leadership. As the transition from laissez-faire to monopoly capitalism was occurring, it became increasingly evident that lawyers' values and behavior reflected the interests of the growing capitalistic order—that law was controlled more by the demands of the market place than by the dictates of "blind justice."

NOTES

1. William E. Nelson, "Emerging Notions of Modern Criminal Law in the Pre-Revolutionary Era," in Abraham Goldstein and Joseph Goldstein, *Crime, Law and Society* (New York: Free Press, 1971), p. 85.
2. William Appleman Williams, *The Contours of American History* (Chicago: Quadrangle Books, 1966), p. 234.
3. Quoted in ibid., p. 239.
4. Rush Welter, *The Mind of America* (New York: Columbia, 1975), p. 78.
5. Ibid., p. 80.
6. Ibid., p. 90.
7. Quoted in ibid., p. 99.
8. Samuel Scoville, "The Evolution of Our Criminal Procedure," in *Reform in Administration of Justice* (Philadelphia: American Academy of Political and Social Science, 1914), p. 93.
9. Ibid.
10. Ibid., p. 94.
11. *Select Essays in Anglo-American Legal History,* by various authors, compiled and edited by a Committee of the Association of American Law Schools (Boston: Little, Brown and Co., 1908), p. 521.
12. Ibid.
13. See generally, ibid.
14. Roscoe Pound, *Criminal Justice in America* (New York: Henry Holt and Co., 1930), p. 135.
15. Ibid., p. 136.
16. Ibid., p. 138.
17. Ibid., pp. 138–39.
18. Whitney North Seymour, Jr., *Why Justice Fails* (New York: William Morrow, 1923), p. 2.

19. Pound, *Criminal Justice,* p. 117.

20. Ibid., p. 130.

21. Ibid.

22. Edwin H. Sutherland, *Criminology* (Philadelphia and London: J. B. Lippincott Co., 1924), p. 262.

23. Ibid.

24. Ibid., p. 261.

25. Nathaniel F. Cantor, *Crime: Criminals, and Criminal Justice* (New York: Henry Holt and Co., 1932), p. 143.

26. Charles D. Edelstein and Robert J. Wicks, *An Introduction to Criminal Justice* (New York: McGraw-Hill, 1977), pp. 6–7.

27. Louis P. Carney, *Introduction to Correctional Science* (New York: McGraw-Hill, 1974), pp. 88–94.

28. Janet Harris, *Crisis in Corrections* (New York: McGraw-Hill, 1973), pp. 37–46.

29. Raymond Moley, "The Vanishing Jury," in *Southern California Law Review* (December 1928), II:2.

30. Edelstein and Wicks, *Introduction to Criminal Justice*, p. 7.

31. Cantor, *Crime: Criminals,* p. 145.

32. Ibid., pp. 143–144.

33. Quoted in "The Municipal Court of Chicago," by J. Kent Greene, *University of Pennsylvania Law Review,* Vol. 58 (1909–10), p. 335.

34. "Efficiency in the Administration of Justice," prepared by Charles W. Eliot, Moorfield Storey, et. al., for the National Economic League, (Pamphlet), (Boston: May 1916).

35. Cantor, *Crime: Criminals,* p. 142.

36. Authur Train, *Courts and Criminals* (New York: Scribner's, 1924), pp. 218–219.

37. Edwin R. Keedy, "The Decline of Traditionalism and Individualism," *University of Pennsylvania Law Review,* Vol. 65, (1916–1917), p. 776.

38. Quoted from an address to the president and members of the bar association of San Francisco on October 13, 1910, in *The Bar Association of San Francisco: The First Hundred Years* (1872–1972), Kenneth M. Johnson (San Francisco: Recorder Printing and Publishing Co., 1972), pp. 42–43.

39. Train, *Courts and Criminals,* pp. 215–216.

40. Pound, *Criminal Justice,* p. 162.

41. Ibid., p. 25.

42. Train, *Courts and Criminals,* p. 217.

43. Scoville, "Evolution of Our Criminal Procedure," pp. 95–96.

44. Cantor, *Crime: Criminals,* p. 181.

45. Ibid., pp. 180–181.

46. William E. Mikell, "Criminal Procedure—Defects in its Administration," *The Annals of the American Academy of Political and Social Science,* Vol. 125–126, (May–July 1926), p. 95.

47. Quoted in Johnson, *Bar Association of San Francisco,* p. 44.

48. Cantor, *Crime, Criminals,* p. 143.

49. Johnson, *Bar Association of San Francisco,* p. 40.

50. Ibid., p. 35.
51. Ibid., p. 38.
52. Mikell, "Criminal Procedure," p. 90.
53. Eliot, Storey, et. al., "Efficiency in Administration," p. 11.
54. Pound, *Criminal Justice,* p. 76.
55. Ibid.
56. Ibid., pp. 177–178.
57. Quoted in Johnson, *Bar Association of San Francisco,* p. 43.

2 STATUS / POLITICS / CLASS: The Profession

In the late 1700's and early 1800's, the power to control trials passed from judges to lawyers who, with or without qualifications, were practicing criminal law. What emerged was an informal courtroom in which attorneys conducted trials before spectators and jurors while judges, some lay and some not, acted as umpires or referees.

The prosecutor for a local community was expected to fulfill the roles of criminal investigator and common-law attorney-general. He also had to decide whether or not a case should be prosecuted, prepare a case for trial, and then actually try the case. At times he even had to serve as the representative counsel for the defense.

Before the Voluntary Defender System and the Public Defender System were established, the prosecutor (acting as both a public agent and a judicial officer) was also expected to perform the contradictory tasks of impartially weighing the evidence and prosecuting the guilty while protecting the innocent. For at least three reasons prosecutors found it difficult to remain impartial: first, he was an elected officer who attracted votes based on the number of convictions he could report; second, the court had a vested interest in convictions; and third, the prosecutor found himself in combat with lawyers who were employing all their skills to acquit their clients.

The prosecuting office was also immersed in politics. As Cantor notes, "the ease with which corrupt political organizations can control the prosecutor's office is partially explained by the striking decentralization of that office."[1]

Prosecutors sought to enhance their professional reputation and acheive political names for themselves by: (1) fixing cases through prosecutorial discretion (e.g., no papers, *nolle prosequi,* discharge, and want of prosecution); (2) by plea bargaining to obtain guilty pleas; and (3) by conducting prosecutions in an overly enthusiastic manner in order to secure high conviction rates. Such prosecutorial activities were often the grounds for mistrials and reversals:

> The law abounds with numerous decisions in which appellate tribunals have reversed convictions and granted new trials on account of improprieties, prejudice, or misconduct of district attorneys.[2]

Writing about the intimacy between politics and prosecutors, Pound asserted that prosecutors were inadequate for typical cases coming to the attention of the criminal court:

> Prosecutors publish statements showing 'convictions' running to thousands each year. But more than ninety percent of these 'convictions,' are upon pleas of guilty, made on 'bargain days,' in the assured expectation of nominal punishment, as the cheapest way out, and amounting in effect to license to violate the law. The political value of sensation and the danger of offending those on whose political favor he must depend for political advancement are not unlikely to drive him to a perfunctory routine for his ordinary work and spectacular handling of a few sensational cases.[3]

Both J. M. Maguire, author of *The Lance of Justice: A Semi-Centennial History of the Legal Aid Society* (1876–1926),[4] and Professor Raymond of Columbia Law School, who was associated with the famous crime surveys of the early twenties, wrote that the strong political nature of the prosecutorial office often resulted in an erratically applied criminal law and an inefficient and inexact policy concerning prosecution:

> The power which he [the prosecutor] thus finds ready to his hand is exercised within the scope of ample discretion. Cases are dropped how, when, and why he decrees. His discretion, moreover, is exercised within the protective darkness of inadequate records and reports. He is not subject to any important extent to the restraining influences of public and professional scrutiny. Most important of

all, the office thus vested with power is, in reality, sought and used for purposes of partisan politics.[5]

In spite of the political purposes served by the district attorney, prosecutorial practices went unchallenged. The chances, then, of a prosecutor fulfilling the role of a judicial officer who protects the rights of the innocent, let alone the guilty, were slim.

During most of the nineteenth century, there was competent defense for those who could afford it. With the rise of corporate law and business law, however, there was a gradual decline in the caliber of lawyers practicing criminal law. By the end of the century the most highly skilled lawyers had abandoned criminal law altogether (i.e., "the best-trained element of the bar more and more does its chief work out of court, and almost wholly avoids criminal cases"[6]).

Among the young who became skilled and successful practitioners, some remained in criminal law, but the majority went into an area of civil practice. Typically, young and inexperienced or older and unsuccessful lawyers found work at the expense of the poor. Unethical lawyers, referred to as "shysters," or "ambulance chasers," preyed on poor defendants for their survival within the legal profession. Defendants such as migrant workers, immigrants, and blacks were, with the exception of murder trials, rushed through the courts with scant attention given to their cases. As far as indigents were concerned, they had little hope of being defended at all.

Lawyers in Colonial America

Because the American colonies were rudimentary communities with simple economies, there was little need for law and lawyers. Also, because there was little money to be made in either criminal or civil law, lawyers held a fairly insignificant position during the earlier colonial period.

There are two reasons why lawyers were unpopular during the first hundred years of colonial America. First, lawyers were viewed by wealthy merchants, landed aristocracy, clergymen, and royal governors as potential threats to their political oligarchy in the New World. It was not uncommon for these powerful figures to position themselves as deputy sheriffs, justices, and even county clerks. Because these groups had a great influence on the courts, lawyers, if they did not "cooperate," found themselves in a dangerous position. Second, the colonists regarded law and the practice of law as antiquated and tyrannical; a rigid legal system contrasted with the prevailing spirit of individualism and dissent. Lawyers in particular were regarded contemptuously by the colonists; they were despised because they helped to maintain the inequities of common law. Also, negative opinions of the legal profession were encouraged because the lawyers were largely untrained and unskilled.

From the middle of the seventeenth to the middle of the eighteenth century, lawyers faced hostile legislation. Legislation limited the number of times a court could be in session and even restricted the use of lawyers. For example:

> In 1642–43, an Act for the Better Regulation of Attorneys forbade pleading causes for another without license from the court where one pleads and provided that one was not to have such license from more than two courts, the Quarter Court and one County Court.[7]

In the case of general jurisdiction of first instance, the County Court met from six to twelve times a year. The Quarter Court, as the name implies, met four times a year to dispose of all appropriate judicial business. Therefore, a lawyer could not expect to make a living with so little time allotted to the practice of advocation and litigation.

In addition to the short time allotted to courtroom appearances, legislation established fixed fees, and heavy penalties were incurred if a lawyer charged more than a fixed fee. Furthermore, a lawyer had little opportunity for fee negotiations because he could not refuse a retainer unless he was already retained by the other side of the same controversy. Another act maintained that:

> Many troublesome suits have multiplied by the unskillfulness and

covetousness of attorneys and provides that all 'mercenary attorneys' be 'wholly expelled from that office'. except as to cases already undertaken or depending.[8]

And still another act in 1656 provided that only lawyers who qualified by the laws of England as "counsellors at law" would be accorded all the corresponding privileges.[9] Thus, in Virginia the practice of law was limited to those lawyers who had been admitted as Barristers by the Inns of Court. Even worse, from 1658 to 1682, Virginia forbade any person from pleading for or giving counsel in any cause or controversy for a fee, either directly or indirectly.[10] This act was repealed in 1682, but the statutory regulation of fees continued until 1849.[11]

The last quarter of the seventeeth century in colonial America witnessed a change in attitudes toward lawyers as a social class. The change occurred because colonists recognized the futility of forbidding representation in litigation, as well as the inefficiency of every man attempting to be his own attorney. The time had arrived when the number of drafting instruments, contracts, deeds, and wills was too large to leave in the hands of laymen who possessed little if any competence or training in the law. In addition, the practice of court officials acting as attorneys in their respective courts was beginning to annoy many dissatisfied clients. Most importantly, the colonists began to resent all the legal work which, out of necessity, was being conducted by nonprofessionals of the court. These nonprofessionals were the petty practitioners and mercenary attorneys who often drummed up unsavory and ridiculous litigation.[12]

John Adams in his autobiography mentions his attempt to stop the abuses of pettifoggers and amateurs who frequently drew up wrong writs, stirred up unnecessary suits, and received the fees established for lawyers. To put an end to the practice of law by nonlawyers, New York, in 1683, followed by other colonies, passed legislation which forbade not only pettifoggers and sharpers from practicing law, but also prevented sheriffs, constables, clerks, and justices of the peace from acting as attorneys.[13]

The beginning of the eighteenth century marked a time in which colonies established a system of courts where justice was administered according to the law. By 1725 the courts in the colonies of Virginia, Massachusetts, Maryland, Pennsylvania, New Jersey, and South Carolina had made the change. In each colony there existed courts that:

> Required trained and responsible agents for litigation and advocates, and there came to be systems of prescribed qualifications of admission to practice, and of responsibility of the practitioners.[14]

During the eighteenth century, the status of the law and lawyers changed from one of minimal significance to one of great importance. The change in status was due to changing economic conditions and their influence on the development of noncriminal law.

A mercantile system of capitalism was emerging; commerce, export trade, ship building, fishing, and slave trading became big businesses. As a consequence, rich merchants were concerned with increasingly complex business contracts, papers, land rights, and wills. Skilled lawyers were needed to answer all types of legal questions dealing with business affairs. Recognizing the growing importance of the legal profession, the wealthy classes began to send their sons to England's Inns of Court. Also, American colleges began to concentrate on upgrading their programs of legal education. Between 1750 and 1775, colleges such as Harvard, Yale, and William and Mary had achieved equal status with England in legal education.

The prestige of the legal profession was further enhanced by the Revolutionary War. Lawyers were the most represented group of spokesmen, writers, and orators for the colonists against the mother country. Although some of the most influential lawyers sided with the royalists, the majority of lawyers of this period shared in the planning of American independence.

Lawyers from the Revolution to the Civil War

According to Roscoe Pound, the formative era in the development of American law, legal institutions, and the legal profession was the period between the American Revolution and the Civil War. The Revolutionary War brought about tremendous changes in American society. Social and financial conditions were in a state of unrest; businesses had been interrupted, prices had risen, and public debts had climbed. The collecting of debts, the enforcing of contracts, and the foreclosing of countless mortgages were carried out by lawyers.

Despite the increasingly important role played by lawyers and the growth of federal bars (composed primarily of lawyers from Pennsylvania, Maryland, and Virginia) between 1789 and 1812, local bars and benches did not organize. Economic, political, and social factors obstructed the growth and progress of the American legal profession during this time.

The worsening economic conditions had the greatest impact on the character of the legal profession during the turn of the nineteenth century. Business was disturbed not only by the large number of public and private debts as a result of the Revolution, but also by the closing of ports and by the British Navigation Acts that closed off profitable trade with the West Indies.

During this period a primary task of lawyers was to collect bills. People resented lawyers not only for this onerous task, but also because lawyers were kept busy litigating and advocating in courts while everyone else was unemployed. Lawyers were also criticized for refusing to work without an advanced retainer (the government's paper money was practically worthless and therefore few people had good credit). Pound explains:

> The Tories were reclaiming their property under the treaty of peace, and English creditors were seeking to recover the debts due them in spite of confiscatory legislations. Those were the days of strict foreclosures and imprisonment for debts. The chief law business was collection of debts and recovery of property held under confiscatory law.[15]

Shays' Rebellion in Massachusetts testified to the strong sentiments against the legal profession. The rebellion was aimed at lawyers, judges, and courtrooms. Similar protests prevailed in other states. For example, debtors in Vermont set fire to court houses while people in New Jersey simply boarded and nailed up the doors to the courts. In each of these places both lawyers and judges were mobbed and their lives threatened.[16]

After the war, attitudes were negative toward lawyers trained in the common law. Similarly, the English law was held in disdain. Moreover, the period of distrust toward England and the common law was extended by the spirit of Jeffersonian democracy. The period has been characterized by such noted scholars as Alexis DeTocqueville, in *Democracy in America,* and Charles A. Beard, in *The Rise of American Civilization,* as one fixed upon notions of democracy, equality, and the unity of all American people. The ideas of professionalism were diametrically opposed to Jeffersonian ideals. To dignify one calling as professional and another as nonprofessional was considered undemocratic. The general sentiment was to open the practice of law to everyone, contrary to the English preference for a restricted, organized, and self-regulating profession. Consequently, the American legal profession suffered from the participation of unskilled and untrained men professing to be lawyers.

In response to the anti-British climate, some of the older and more conservative lawyers of the pre-revolutionary days were either leaving the country or, as honest loyalists, ceasing to practice. At the same time, many lawyers were bitter soldiers returning from war. They possessed little knowledge of the law, but were anxious to make money in the land for which they had fought.[17] This type of lawyer only contributed more to the negative images of the legal profession and added to the dissatisfaction with the administration of justice.

Another factor that contributed to the decline of the legal profession was the decentralization of judicial administration. Long distances between towns forced the establishment of many independent courts of general jurisdiction. "Regulars" began frequenting the local courts and made up the unofficial bars of these small town communities. In addition, as Esther Brown wrote:

> The jealousy of the individual states over any infringement of their jurisdiction by the federal government further accentuated the difficulties of the legal profession.[18]

Until the War of 1812, the legal profession was struggling desperately to regain the public esteem that had been so laboriously achieved at the time of the Revolutionary War. The cycle was complete: the elite-dominated legal profession of the late eighteenth century had reverted to a lowly skilled group of practitioners, as it had been during the seventeenth and greater part of the eighteenth centuries.

Lawyers in the Industrial Revolution

The Industrial Revolution, sparked by the War of 1812, altered both the content and practice of the law. The following quote illuminates the dynamic interchange between economic expansion and the development of the legal profession:

> The War of 1812 exercised a great influence upon economic and legal history. It gave rise to a vast number of decisions on prize and admiralty law. It turned attention, which had been centered almost exclusively upon shipping and agriculture, to manufacture and invention. As a result, corporation and patent law made their appearance. Because coastwide trade was ruined by the British blockade, the war promoted the construction of canals, turnpikes, and better means of internal communication. Increased transportation resulted in opening new areas for legal service.[19]

Industrialism provided many opportunities for ambitious lawyers. Some of the best lawyers of this period dropped criminal law practices altogether because of the monetary or political advantages associated with business law. Those lawyers specifically skilled in courtroom advocacy appeared less and less in litigation. Instead, these lawyers, as representatives of business, took on the role of client-caretaker or legal advisor. At this point, the traditional responsibility of the lawyer to indicate to his clients whether or not their interests complied with the law was altered. Instead, after the Industrial Revolution, lawyers were more concerned with creating new laws and changing the old so that the law would comply with the interests of their clients.

Corporate lawyers composed an aristocratic professional class. To those people who had grown up during the Jeffersonian era or who were experiencing the Jacksonian era, the idea of an aristocratic bar was received antagonistically. The following are quotes used by Pound to document the pioneer-spirited American attitude toward aristocratic lawyers:

Benjamin Austin, the anti-federalist politician of Boston, referring to the "order of lawyers" wrote:

> The order is becoming continually more and more powerful. . . .
> There is danger of lawyers becoming powerful as a combined body.
> The people should be guarded against it as it might subvert every
> principle of law and establish a perfect aristocracy. . . . This order
> of men should be annihilated.

In Philadelphia William Duane, editor of the *Aurora,* the organ of Jefferson's party, was no less vigorous in his attacks upon the bar as a "privileged order or class."

In the early 1800's Jared Ingersoll of Philadelphia wrote "our State rulers threaten to lop away that excrescense on civilization, the Bar."

As it has been written, "The bar was regarded as too aristocratic, the law was deemed too feudal."

Another writer denounced Bar Associations as being "wrong in principle, betray[ing] competition, delay[ing] professional freedom, degrad[ing] the bar as a 'secret trade union.' "[20]

The fact that the legal profession was splintered left its impact on the administration of criminal justice. The practice of law inside courtrooms, especially criminal courts, depreciated. The former checks and balances within the profession disappeared. Consequently, loose and disreputable forensic practices emerged throughout the country, especially in the larger cities. From 1800 to 1860, lawyers were admitted to the bar irrespective of educational background or professional training (apprenticeships). Throughout this period, legislation sought to open up the practice of law by abolishing educational requirements and by either reducing or eliminating the length and quality of professional training.* Because of the lowered requirements for the practice of law, the appearance of unscrupulous lawyers occurred in matters of small, private concerns. Even older reputable attorneys began to lose standing in the community as the entire legal profession's status continued to decline.**

During the latter part of the nineteenth century, then, the precorporate lawyer came into existence, complete with all kinds of resources—from money and manpower to experience and influence. In approximately eighty years, or by the end of the New Deal, lawyers within the upper (corporate) hierarchies of the profession had almost completely abandoned the role of advocate. Instead, these lawyers had become nothing more than an extension of big business management, acting primarily as consultants and lawmakers.[21]

To suggest, however, that economics were totally responsible for the changes occurring within the legal profession before the Civil War would be misleading. The prevailing ideology of the period, "insurgent democracy," also helped

---

* Examples of such legislation are New Hampshire in 1842; all citizens (male) over 21 were eligible (N.H. Rev. Stat. 1842, Ch. 177, Sec. 2); every citizen (male) of Maine in 1843 (Maine, Acts and Resolves of 1843, Chapter 12); every resident (male) of Wisconsin (Laws of 1849, Chapter 152).

** Legislation had changed both the conditions and the composition of the legal profession with respect to admittance: in the year 1800, 14 out of 19 states/territories prescribed a definite period of preparation for admission to the bar; by 1840 only 11 out of 30 did; and by 1860 only 9 out of 39 did. In sixty years the proportion of states/territories requiring preparation had shrunk from 74% to 23%, while the number of states/territories had more than doubled.

bring about changes in the legal profession. At this time, there was a generally negative attitude about governmental privileges. In other words, attacks against elaborate preparation for the practice of law were not a question of isolated hostility and dislike of the profession as in the earlier colonial days, but, rather, were characteristic of the dislike and resentment toward all governmental positions. Generally speaking, qualifications for most governmental officers were reduced at this time. In reference to the movement of deprofessionalization, the Carnegie Foundation's publication, "Training for the Public Profession of the Law," stated:

> The movement was grounded in the political philosophy of an insurgent democracy, which was fighting its way into control of our governmental machinery, and was less concerned with making sure that privileges bestowed by the state should be well bestowed than with guarding against their again becoming a monopoly of a favored class in the community.[22]

Among other factors contributing to the decadence and deprofessionalism of the legal profession were: (1) faith in the natural right of every man to pursue any career of his choice; (2) distrust of specialization and the requirments of special training; and (3) fear of the creation of privileged classes emerging from the recognition of professional statuses. During this period, "the bar was not to be regarded as a profession, with requirments for admission, but as *a mere private, money-making occupation*" (emphasis added).[23]

After the Civil War, the development of the legal profession, as well as the law, became increasingly dependent on the changing economic relationships in society. Industrialization, expanding railroads, reconstruction, the settling of the West, urbanization, immigration, foreign markets, and enlarging world trade all had profound effects on the changing legal institutions and developing legal profession.

Lawyers in Reconstruction and Progressive America

Following the Civil War, both the nature of legal practices and the types of legal services that were needed had changed.* Two complementary trends are discernable during this period: a general movement within the legal profession to advocate less in court while advising legal clients outside of court more often and, at the same time, *independent general practice of three generations earlier was beginning to give way to specialization.*

Corporate law was expanding enormously. A growing number of lawyers were employed by industrial or commercial concerns on either a salary or retainer basis. Furthermore, the development of big business in the second half of the nineteenth century not only changed the organization of the legal profession, but also had a strong impact on the operation and structure of legal institutions in general.

The legal profession was affected by the growth of large cities and an increase in the number of courts sitting. These courts were neither unified nor coordinated adequately enough to control the conduct of lawyers practicing in them. Other checks and balances that had informally operated to bring pressure on individual lawyers had ceased to be effective deterrents on professional conduct.

Structurally, the changing political economy also caused an imbalance in the power structures within the legal profession. The field of corporate law was expanding and creating lucrative positions for aspiring lawyers. As a consequence, there was a greater concentration of power among members of the corporate bar. At the same time, as the influence of law in corporate matters was mushrooming, the strength of lawyers who remained in the public sector was dwindling. At a time of increased class conflict and chaotic social conditions, lawyers outside of corporate law lacked both power and influence. In other words, while corporate lawyers were involved in the economic impetus of the growing capitalistic order, the legal profession as a whole lacked

---

* Throughout this discussion and others which follow, the author maintains the position that the types of practices available are in response to the types of services needed. Furthermore, that the types of services needed are influenced most strongly by the changing economic relationships in society.

the influence to address effectively the serious deficiencies in the social and political policies of the times. Instead, effort was directed toward covering up substantive issues by advocating "easy" reforms for the more obvious weaknesses of the social order and of the criminal justice system (e.g., Public Defender System, Juvenile Justice System, indeterminate sentence). Because these reforms did little to alleviate the real problems of the American public, the reputation of the legal profession was severely undermined.

Most lawyers of reputation and skill, excluding those preoccupied with scholarly pursuits, were concerning themselves less and less with community problems. The miscellaneous interests of society were becoming subservient to the interests of the high paying corporate clients. As Louis D. Brandeis said in 1905:

> The leaders of the bar have, with a few exceptions, not only failed to take part in constructive legislation designed to solve in the public interest our great social, economic and industrial problems; but they have failed likewise to oppose legislation prompted by selfish interest. They have often gone further in disregard of the common wealth. They have often advocated, as lawyers, legislative measures which as citizens they could not approve, and have endeavored to justify themselves by a false analogy. *They have erroneously assumed that the rule of ethics to be applied to a lawyer's advocacy is the same where he acts for private interests against the public as it is in litigation between private individuals* (emphasis added.)[24]

To the constituency of corporate lawyers, the quality of the criminal courts, the adjustment of small claims, and the unremunerative litigation of the poor was of no concern, except in the case where changes or reforms were consistent with the needs of big business. Mr. Justice Stone at a dedication referred to the alliance between lawyers and business:

> At its best the changed system has brought to the command of the business world loyalty and superb proficiency and technical skill. At its worst it had made the learned profession of an earlier day the obsequious servant of business, and tainted it with the morals and manners of the market place in its most antisocial manifestations.[25]

To keep in step with the traditional interpretation of justice, the legal profession was involved with notions of the "law" rather than with notions of "justice"; more succinctly, the administration of justice was subordinate to the administration of the law.

The emphasis on the law over justice permitted members of the legal profession to neglect social responsibilities. An article entitled, "The Bar Specializes—With What Results?" states that:

> A large number of the most ingenious and capable attorneys have deserted the fields where their predecessors once rendered a very necessary service to society in general, in order to devote themselves to the remaking of old tools, techniques, and institutions to serve the needs of large scale business and finance.[26]

This devotion of lawyers to the needs of the market place enabled many businessmen to accumulate great wealth at the expense of the general public.

The emerging preference of the leaders of the profession to be involved with corporate, rather than individual, concerns spread throughout the bar. The dollar became the symbol of success and the mercenary attitude of the corporate lawyer (who epitomized the most prestigious members of the legal profession) permeated the bar. The outcome was that public service and welfare law became largely devoid of meaning. In 1938 Esther Brown asserted that:

> The number of competent and honest lawyers willing to struggle for civil liberties and personal rights rather than property rights, and to care for the interests of the poor and of the persons of inadequate means is distressingly small.[27]

Similarly, Newman Levy, a New York attorney, wrote in 1927:

> There is no other profession quite so smug and selfsatisfied, and at the same time quite so lacking in social obligation. An occasional rare soul, a Clarence Darrow, may dedicate his energies to the defense of unpopular causes and earn the supercilious disapproval of his more orthodox brethren. Here and there in the courts may be found some obscure lawyer battling for the poor, the needy, and the oppressed without regard for the pecuniary rewards that spell professional success. But these are the freaks of the profession;

they are, to use that most devastating epithet, the radicals. Most lawyers prefer to seek the more comfortable and reputable rewards of pecuniary success.[28]

Thus, the motivation behind lawyers' decisions to take a case was not legal ethics, but legal retainers. The concern for social justice or the protection of the indigent accused of a crime was too costly for the "successful" lawyer to sacrifice his time and money. Hence, the practice of criminal law was left in the hands of the less powerful lawyers, including many unscrupulous practitioners merely trying to make a living.

The early years of the twentieth century mark the appearance of various federal and state boards, commissions, and bureaus (e.g., antitrust, food and drug, labor safety) and the accompanying expansion of administrative law. The increased participation of government in regulatory matters has had a double effect on the legal profession: first, the various governmental agencies began to incorporate the talents of people trained in the law, whether in official or unofficial capacities; and second, there was the birth of the Washington Law Firms, which represented the multicorporate interests in their struggle with regulatory agencies.

Although the areas of administrative law were growing and developing, other areas of the law, especially quasi-legal matters, were shrinking. New professions were engaging in activities previously conducted by lawyers. For example:

Title examination and conveyancing, which once occupied a large proportion of an attorney's time, [were] gradually being taken from him by the spread of title insurance and by decrease in number of persons holding real estate. Banks and trust companies [were] persistently invading the field of administration and management of estates that lawyers once found profitable. Industrial compensation and liability insurance [had] largely eliminated certain former sources of income. The probation system and penal boards of various kinds are reducing the need for legal service. Preparation of income tax returns and other documents . . . have been taken over in part by specialists without law school training.[29]

Also, the lawyer's domain was threatened by the competition of other rapidly developing professions. The position of corporate businessmen as leaders in public administration especially threatened the status of the legal profession.

The legal profession as a whole was in a transitional phase. A major division was taking place within the profession. Between 1891 and 1901 the bar split into two groups: one incorporated and syndicated as a part of the business world; another unincorporated and individualized as an independent legal profession. As a consequence of this split, the individual practitioner had fewer clients, as the incorporated and syndicated lawyers began to monopolize the greater part of all legal transactions.

Lawyers devoted to business causes became specialists rather than general practitioners. The legal business of a growing corporate economy necessitated diversified types of practices, according to the particular needs of big business, such as the handling of trusts, the solving of tax problems, and the obtaining of special legislation. Thus, legal services provided to the "owners of production" increased efficiency. The same was not true of the general public. Private people received poor legal service; the "lump proletariat," none at all.

For the corporate lawyers, the institution of legal representation and advocacy (consistent with legal ethics and canons) was usurped by the interests of business. The lawyers' responsibility of showing their clients how to comply with the law was antiquated. Big business was in need of legal technicians proficient in the art of making, changing, and adjusting the law to coincide with the demands of profit.

Accordingly, corporations began to create legal staffs within their own organizational structures. As a result of the incorporation of lawyers, George Shelton wrote about the corrosion and violation of professional ethics:

> The attorney loses his regard for the integrity of the court. He seeks to triumph by means that no zeal can justify. He betrays his trust as a sworn officer of the court.

Shelton continues:

> All that is essential to the business lawyer is an abundance of
> books, shrewd and alert solicitors for business, and the qualities
> that go to make success in the market. Clerks do most of the work.
> Men of large enterprises and great business corporations have in
> their employment lawyers who occupy the same position as other
> employees and are essentially hired men, paid to do the legal work
> of the employer as the engineer is employed to run the engine or
> the bookkeeper to keep the books.[30]

And, in "The Passing of the Legal Profession," George Bristol's closing remarks for the *Yale Law Journal* of 1912-13 reveal a similar picture:

> And, my good brothers in law, you who are still within the pale of
> the profession, unincorporated and free to think for yourselves,
> how do you like it? Shall we continue to practice law as a profes-
> sion, honor its traditions, cherish and live up to its high ideals, and
> die poor, or shall we fall in line with our more progressive brothers,
> pass over into the business world—incorporated—exploit the pub-
> lic—and live rich?[31]

Another structural change within the legal profession was the emergence of the "law factories," or large-scale legal firms. Corporate lawyers, first in the area of title business, and later in the areas of trusts, escrows, mortgages, loans, and taxes, came together in the spirit of the "division of labor" which had successfully benefited big business, *a la Taylorism*.[32] Emulating the ways of big business, a system of organization was designed which introduced the effectiveness of the specialization and coordination of varied tasks. Thus, individuals with assorted skills and talents, legal and non-legal, were subdivided into particular roles required to perform the most economical and efficient service in the practice of the law. After all: "The hurry of business requires speedy results. Labor-saving methods are demanded, so that busy practitioners can economize their time."[33] And in another article, "The Economic Basis for a Society of Advocates in the City of Chicago," written in 1914, we are told that the solution to the problems of inefficiency and high costs within the area of business law rested with the principles of elementary business.

What was happening to the other members of the legal profession, those individuals who remained unincorporated and independent? Quoting R. Platt:

> The alternatives offered to a lawyer who, by temperament or necessity cannot or will not abandon his profession, are either to abandon the large centers of population for the country town, where the individual practitioner is still a potent force, or accept a salary of the syndicate position with its rank equalling only that of an expert accountant or salesman ... [34]

However, there were many lawyers who remained within the cities, unincorporated and independent. These lawyers found themselves struggling to make a living. They were forced to compete against one another for the scarce and unremunerative legal work left to them by the corporate staffed or retained attorneys. The solo practitioner was also at a disadvantage because of the low requirements for admission to the bar at that time. Thus, the noncorporate sector of the legal profession was filled with unskilled and untrained, often unscrupulous and dishonest individuals that called themselves lawyers.

"Shysters" pervaded the noncorporate areas of the law, but nowhere was their presence greater than in the practice of criminal law. All lawyers, because of economic conditions, rationalized and justified their conduct, ethical and unethical, as being consistent with that of the most successful members of the profession who were either working for or on behalf of large corporations. Shelton wrote as early as 1900: "His [the lawyer's] motives are as solid and his activities as mercenary as can be found in any other occupation, and the business lawyer is the prevailing type of success." [35]

Between 1890 and 1920, the legal profession reflected the interests of monopoly capitalism—legal ideals became market ideals as well. Bristol informs us that:

> The practice of law has been commercialized. It has been transformed from a profession to a business, and a hustling business at that. Financial interests have looked upon the legal profession with longing eyes, and have gradually corralled it and brought it under their domination for the profits which can be acquired by it. [36]

And, as Shelton wrote:

> The learned gentleman of the bar, courteous, of polished manners
> and polite address, is obsolete. The active attorney, shrewd and un-
> scrupulous, rude in manner, not too learned, content with existing
> conditions, a devotee of mannon, whose best is always at the com-
> mand of money, is the prevailing type.[37]

Lawyers in American society, between 1860 and 1930, experienced low public esteem. Public attitudes toward the legal
profession were soured by the business-oriented, public-
blinded, and mercenary practices of lawyers. More important than the status deprivation was the loss of power and
influence accorded the bar due to their growing economic
dependence on monopoly capitalism.

Stimulated by the corruption and misconduct of judges,
lawyers, and various other court and political officials involved in the scandalous practices that characterized the administration of justice, seventy-five attorneys from twenty-
one states met in Saratoga, New York, and formed the ABA
(American Bar Association) in 1878. Writing of the formation of the ABA, Pound cites a Mr. Evarts, who maintained
that scandals such as the Tweed frauds and Erie Railroad
litigation had promoted the organization of this association
to "restore the honor, integrity, and fame of the profession."[38] And Brown wrote:

> According to the constitution that was adopted, the new body had
> five objects: to uphold the honor of the profession, encourage cor-
> dial intercourse, promote the administration of justice, advance
> the science of jurisprudence, and promote uniform legislation
> throughout the United States.[39]

Motivated by the formation of the ABA and by The Association of the Bar of the City of New York, formed in 1870,
the modern era of bar associations began on a nationwide
basis.* The legal profession began to organize itself into col-

---

* Bar associations actually began to develop after the Revolutionary War. However, by the time the War of 1812 had come to an end, these early associations had
either disappeared or lost their influence over lawyers' conduct.

lective bodies for the purposes of "interests" and "services."** Pound has defined bar associations as "a definite and permanent organization of lawyers for purposes of the profession."[40] Agreeing with Pound, most bar associations suggested two general reasons for their formation—to develop good fellowship among the members of the legal profession and to promote social purposes. The following are the general reasons for organizing given by the major bar associations that developed at this time:

> The Association is established to maintain the honor and dignity of the profession, to cultivate social intercourse among its members, and to increase its usefulness in promoting the due administration of justice.[41]

> Maintaining the honor and dignity of the profession of the law, and cultivating social relations among its members, and increasing its usefulness in promoting the due administration of justice.[42]

> To maintain the honor and dignity of the profession of the law, to cultivate social intercourse and acquaintance among members of the Bar, and to increase the usefulness of its members by aiding in the administration of justice and in the promotion of legal and judicial reforms.[43]

The bar associations themselves, regardless of what they espoused, have not escaped criticism. As late as 1930, some 27,000 persons (only 17 percent of all those practicing law) belonged to the ABA.[44] And, referring to the composition of the ABA, Brown wrote, "It has frequently been criticized, both by lawyers and the public, on the ground that it is composed chiefly of the financially more successful lawyers."[45] Brown quotes Representative Benjamin Rosenthal (D., N.Y.) to make evident the close connection of the ABA to the business world:

> Of the 410 lawyers who were members of consumer-related ABA committees in 1970," says Representative Benjamin Rosenthal (D.,

---

** The following are just some of the associations which formed in the seventies: (1) The Bar Association of the City of New York (1870); (2) Cincinnati Bar Association (1872); (3) Iowa State Bar Association (1874); (4) The Bar Association of the City of Boston (1874); and (5) New York State Bar Association (1876).

N.Y.), "only five derived their principal income from the academic community and none, to the best of my knowledge, were members of public-interest law firms." For example, Rosenthal ticked off the 1970 affiliations of the members of the ABA's Division of Food, Drug and Cosmetic Law:

"The vice chairman of the division was general counsel and vice president of the manufacturer of Hellman's Mayonnaise, Mazola Corn Oil and other food products; the secretary was vice president and general counsel for a major drug manufacturer; the chairman of the standing committee on food additives was employed by a manufacturer of food additives and pharmaceuticals; the chairman of the drug law committee was employed by the Pharmaceutical Manufacturers Association; the chairman of the committee on beverage law was in the legal department of Coca-Cola."[46]

Thus, although a great amount of time and energy was spent in an effort to improve the qualifications and training of the profession, little effective control over professional ethics and conduct existed. For example, the ABA in 1893 formed the Committee on Legal Education and Admissions to the Bar; but in 1917, after negligible accomplishments, the committee was abolished. Brown wrote of the ABA that:

In spite of the fact that it had been in existence for over half a century, it had exerted relatively little control over professional matters.[47]

At the time of the emergence of the public defender idea (1898), the members of the legal profession had been stratified according to their relationship with the means of production. The metropolitan centers of the U.S. were witnessing the early stratification of lawyers into four types of practitioners; (1) client-caretakers; (2) defendant lawyers; (3) plaintiff lawyers; and (4) practitioners in criminal cases. (In terms of importance, these unofficial categories of lawyers may be thought of in descending order, as measured by the proportion of attorneys found in each group.)

In part, the inefficiency and high costs of the administration of criminal justice were attributed to the stratification of lawyers. The growing influence of business on the practice of all areas of the law resulted in an enormous amount of public hostility, economic dependence, and a lowered status for the legal profession. Consequently, lawyers, at least those within the financial world, came together in an attempt to restore the status and power of the profession.[48] Although bar associations accomplished little in the areas of restoring power and status, they were able to successfully participate in the "reforming" of the criminal justice system during the Progressive Era.

NOTES

1. Nathaniel E. Cantor, *Crime: Criminals and Criminal Justice* (New York: Henry Holt and Co., 1932), p. 188.
2. Mayer C. Goldman, *The Public Defender: A Necessary Factor in the Administration of Justice* (New York: The Knickerbocker Press, 1917), p. 28.
3. Roscoe Pound, *Criminal Justice in America* (New York: Henry Holt and Co., 1930), p. 184.
4. John MacArthur Maguire, *The Lance of Justice: A Semi-Centennial History of the Legal Aid Society (1876–1926)* (Cambridge: Harvard University Press, 1928), see generally.
5. Quoted in Cantor, *Crime: Criminals,* p. 186.
6. Goldman, *Public Defender,* p. 46.
7. Roscoe Pound, *The Lawyer from Antiquity to Modern Times* (St. Paul: West Publishing Co., 1953), p. 136.
8. Quoted in ibid., p. 142.
9. Quoted in ibid., p. 138.
10. Ibid., p. 136.
11. Ibid., p. 142.
12. John Barbie Minor, *Institutes of Common and Statute Law,* 3rd ed. (1893), IV, p. 203.
13. Quoted in Pound, *The Lawyer from Antiquity,* p. 143.
14. Ibid., p. 145.
15. Ibid., p. 179.
16. Esther Lucille Brown, *Lawyers and the Promotion of Justice* (New York: Russell Sage Foundation, 1938), pp. 11–12.
17. Pound, *The Lawyer from Antiquity,* pp. 232–242.
18. Brown, *Lawyers,* p. 17.
19. Ibid., p. 18.
20. Pound, *The Lawyer from Antiquity,* pp. 232–242.

21. *See* Joseph C. Goulden, *The Super-Lawyers: The Small and Powerful World of the Great Washington Law Firms* (New York: Weybright and Talley, 1971), for an excellent account of the role the "Super-lawyers" have played in the merging of big business and government into a "regulated corporate monopoly."

22. "Training for the Public Profession of the Law," *The Carnegie Foundation for the Advancement of Teaching,* Bulletin 15 (1921), pp. 86–87.

23. Pound, *The Lawyer from Antiquity,* p. 232.

24. Goulden, *Super Lawyers,* p. 232.

25. Harlin F. Stone, "The Public Influence of the Bar," *Harvard Law Review* (November 1930), p. 7.

26. Karl Llewellyn, "The Bar Specializes—With What Results?" *Annals of the American Academy of Political and Social Science* (May 1933), pp. 177–192; See also Maurice Wormser's "Legal Ethics in Theory and in Practice," *The Annals* (May 1933), pp. 196–197.

27. Brown, *Lawyers,* p. 222.

28. Newman Levy, "Lawyers and Morals," *Harper's Magazine,* February 1927, pp. 293–94.

29. Brown, *Lawyers,* p. 20. *See also* James Grafton Rogers, "Forces Remolding the Lawyer's Life," *American Bar Association Journal* (October 1931), pp. 28–37.

30. George F. Shelton, "Law as Business," *Yale Law Journal,* X (1900–1901), pp. 280–281.

31. George W. Bristol, "The Passing of the Legal Profession," *Yale Law Journal,* XXII (1913–1914), p. 613.

32. *See* Frederick W. Taylor, *Scientific Management* (New York: Harper and Row, 1911).

33. Shelton, "Law as Business," p. 276.

34. Robert T. Platt, "The Decadence of Law as a Profession and Its Growth as a Business," *Yale Law Journal,* XII, p. 444.

35. Shelton, "Law as Business," p. 275.

36. Bristol, "Passing of Legal Profession," p. 590.

37. Shelton, "Law as Business," pp. 278–279.

38. Pound, *The Lawyer from Antiquity,* p. 220.

39. Brown, *Lawyers,* p. 128.

40. Pound, *The Lawyer from Antiquity,* p. 253.

41. Article II of the I Rep. Association of the Bar of the City of New York (1870).

42. The stated purpose of the Bar Association of the State of New Hampshire, incorporated July 2, 1873.

43. The stated purpose of the Cleveland Bar Association formed in 1873.

44. Pound, *The Lawyer from Antiquity,* p. 263.

45. Brown, *Lawyers,* p. 129.

46. Ibid., p. 141.

47. Ibid., p. 129.

48. For an excellent description and analysis of not only this period of the legal profession's history, but also of its development to the present, see Jerold S. Auerbach, *Unequal Justice: Lawyers and Social Change in Modern America* (New York: Oxford University Press, 1977).

3 THE PUBLIC DEFENDER: Reformation

Liberal Reformism and the Administration of Criminal Justice

> The tremendous and highly complex industrial development which went on with ever-accelerated rapidity during the latter-half of the nineteenth century brings us face to face, at the beginning of the twentieth, with very serious social problems. The old laws, and the old customs . . . are no longer sufficient.[1]

The social problems of 1901 that Theodore Roosevelt refers to included economic instability, large scale unemployment, severe urban poverty, corruption in politics, labor strikes, lenient immigration codes, rising criminality, and spirited movements demanding alternative social systems to replace the dying political economy of nineteenth century laissez-faire capitalism. The laws and the customs referred to included the substantive as well as the procedural aspects of the administration of justice and the decaying ideology of "individualism-competitiveness," both of which were ill-adapted to the needs of a changing political economy.

Beginning in the late 1870's, academic circles were already discussing a new ideology that radically differed from laissez-faire capitalism. The traditional role of nineteenth century liberal scholars was being criticized by such noted academicians as Lester Ward (1883), E.A. Ross (1905), William James (1907), and John Dewey (1898).[2] These scholars and others argued for an applied science; no longer were social scientists, economists, and jurists only to observe and formulate the laws of nature, but they were also to experiment and suggest change. Laissez-faire gave way to corporate capitalism, and social Darwinism faded into reform Darwinism; competition and individual efficiency were to be replaced by cooperation and social "efficiency." For example, in the emerging field of criminology, the fatalistic theories (e.g., biological, hereditary) of criminal behavior were being replaced by the new ideas of Enrico Ferri, Baron Raffaele Garofalo, Charles Cooley, and the positivist school of criminal law and criminology. These positivist theories of the nineties argued that "degenerates" could be "reformed" into law-abiding citizens through the power of medical science and rational treatment, aided by an improved, efficient, and humane system of criminal justice.

The law in the twentieth century was witnessing the rise of sociological jurisprudence, the product of the growing popularity of scientism. Traditionally, the law was viewed as impregnable, eternal, and deductive. But, catalyzed by the unorthodox arguments of Holmes and Brandeis, the law came to be conceptualized as perpetually evolving through induced and scientifically managed decisions. Accordingly, with the creation of law, legal scholars, it was thought, would be able to engineer the transformation from a laissez-faire to a planned society. Samuel Mencher in his analysis, *Poor Law to Poverty Program,* writes of this social transformation through the law:

> In the law, philosophy and practice were combined in the leadership of a new group of "social" jurists. Such eminent and influential lawyers and justices as Holmes, Brandeis, Cardoza, and Pound discarded the prevalent fixed and rigid constitutionalism and introduced a socially oriented pragmatism. The State and the courts, in their opinion, should not stand by but protect the interests of individuals and the underprivileged generally in the increasingly unequal struggle against big business and giant organizations. Thus, progress became associated with clearly identifiable objectives to be achieved consciously and actively.[3]

However, Roscoe Pound, the man who is most closely associated with the philosophy of sociological jurisprudence (following in the footsteps of Oliver Wendell Holmes), emphasized throughout his prodigious writings not individual interests, but social interests. Without mention of the struggle against big business, Pound writes:

> I am content to see in legal history the record of a continually wider recognizing and satisfying of human wants or claims or desires through social control; a more embracing and more effective securing of social interests; a continually more complete and effective elimination of waste and precluding of friction in human enjoyment of the goods of existence—in short, a continually more efficacious social engineering.[4]

Generally, the infiltration of the social sciences into the law and the administration of criminal justice occurred during the first three decades of the twentieth century. Numerous articles and treatises with references to extra-legal materials began to appear. Law journals and journals of crime and delinquency (e.g., *The American Institute of Criminal Law and Criminology; The American Judicature Society;* and *The Journal of Criminal Law, Criminology, and Police Science*) began to adopt the languages and models of the disciplines of economics, sociology, psychology, and anthropology. And finally, the various crime surveys and investigative studies of the administrative branches of the law during the twenties did the same. Working with the proposition that the "legal order is a phase of social control," Pound and his followers suggested that the law "to be understood must be taken in its setting among social phenomena;" consequently, he urged "study of the actual social effects of legal institutions and legal doctrines; sociological study in preparation for lawmaking; and study of the means of making legal precepts effective in action."[5] And as Sheldon Glueck wrote about the changing study of the law:

> The significant factor is the radical shift of emphasis and point of view to study of the living matter of litigation; to a 'functional' as well as a 'structural' approach; to investigation of the psychology as well as the anatomy and histology of law as a social institution and an instrument of social control.[6]

In the spirit of sociological jurisprudence, the American Law Institute incorporated on February 22, 1923, with the financial support of the Carnegie Corporation. The expressed purpose of the Institute was "to promote the clarification and simplification of the law and its better adaptation to social needs, to secure the better administration of justice, and to encourage and carry on scholarly and scientific legal work."[7] Nevertheless, social scientists, outside the legal profession, did not participate in the formation of the Institute. And when the Institute, at the request of the American Bar Association, the Association of American Law Schools, and the American Institute of Criminal Law and Criminology, conducted its study of 48 states in order to design their Model Code of Criminal Procedure, Cantor criticized the fact that no behavioral scientists were at hand:

> It is to be regretted, however, that the Institute failed to include on its staff non-legal criminologists. The yeast of broader viewpoints might have given rise to innovations in criminal procedure. The present Code represents a combination of improvements in the present outmoded practice rather than a radical innovation based upon the political, social and legal dynamics of criminal administration.[8]

A survey of the various crime commissions of the twenties (e.g., Cleveland, Michigan) revealed an insignificant proportion of social scientists who were either legal jurists or legal authorities. The conclusions of this survey and Cantor's comments cited above seem to indicate that while the reform ideology of corporate liberalism was espoused, the more important self-serving interests of the law and legal bureaucracies were kept intact.

Criminal Justice Reform: Expediency, Efficiency and Economy

An examination of the psychology, language, and objectives of reformers within the administration of criminal justice reveals a fundamental belief in the prevailing corporate order. Specifically, those reformers involved in the public defender movement, whether interested in and emphasizing humanitarian concern for the poor, or influenced by and preoccupied with strengthening the status quo, all believed in the sanctity of private property and a private (as opposed to a socialized) bar. They also believed in the distinction made between "criminal" and "civil" violations, and the "free-enterprise" system of monopoly capitalism.

The transformation from laissez-faire to monopoly capitalism changed the prevailing ideas about human nature. First, the inadequacies of individualized and random activity were discussed at great length in the spheres of business and government. Spokesmen and directors for the new order called for a cooperative and interrelated system of planned, controlled, and coordinated institutions.[9] Second, competition was regarded as inefficient, redundant, wasteful, and potentially capable of destroying the capitalistic order. What was needed in the place of competition was a routined, ordered, and regulated economy resulting in more efficient management. Third, consistent with the first two points, pragmatism, opportunism, and instrumentalism, as epitomized by the writings of George Herbert Mead and the scientific management of Taylorism, were demanded. The consonant ideas of compromise, accommodation, and the running of the American system as a system were encouraged by such men as Mark Hanna and George W. Perkins of the corporate braintrust. Fourth, the collective appeal of "syndicalism," or the development of a division of labor within the corporate order, established the organization and coordination of separate functional groups. This "syndicalism" was adopted as the governing ideology, harmonizing the common interests shared by class ties.

General trends in social policy, both at home and abroad, were evolving throughout American-controlled institutions. For example, legal reformers, consistent with Theodore Roosevelt and Elihu Root's foreign policy of reform in underdeveloped countries with American interests, desired changes that would provide for (1) security of life and private property through the vigorous punishments of "index" crimes; (2) orderly and certain administration of impartial justice within the criminal law; and (3) power to repress subversive disorder whenever the situation demanded it.[10]

Woodrow Wilson, in 1913, said "We shall deal with our economic system as it is and as it may be modified, not as it might be if we had a clean sheet of paper to write upon."[11] This statement characterizes the basic attempt—moderation and gradualism—of criminal justice reformers to make the appropriate and necessary corrections within that system. Reformers within the criminal justice system operated with the fundamental assumption that the substantive criminal law could be improved through procedural-administrative changes. These reformers acted with the same "syndicalist" logic, but not necessarily the same class-conscious orientation of the leaders in industry and business. Predominantly represented by lawyers and judges, this group of legal reformers was concerned with how the criminal justice system could be more effectively operated and controlled through amelioristic changes designed both to elevate their public image and to make work easier, more efficient, and less costly.

Expediency, efficiency, and economy were the dominant objectives of the reforms that occurred within the administration of the criminal law. Throughout the literature of the period, the theme appears to have been that the basic structure of the law and the system were not the reasons for the breakdown and dissatisfaction with the administration of criminal justice. Instead, blame was to be attributed to court administrators, judges, and lawyers. For example, even after some of the modern codes of criminal procedure had been implemented, the Illinois Crime Survey, conducted in the late 1920's concluded:

> Failures of justice are traceable more often to administrative defects than to weaknesses in the laws. However, I do not mean to depreciate the value of the modern codes of criminal procedure. Changes in laws made with a view to meeting modern conditions of crime and putting the state in criminal prosecutions upon a more even footing with the defendant will be a great help to honest, vigorous, and conscientious administrators of the law, but when

placed in the hands of public officials who are disposed toward laxity of enforcement and leniency towards criminals, they become no more effective than the so-called obsolete criminal codes.[12]

During the first three decades of this century, the credibility as well as the status of the American legal profession was extremely low due to the profession's unsympathetic attitude toward changing social needs and community problems; consequently, in all areas of legal reform, priority was given to raising the profession's image. For example, the San Francisco newspaper, *The Recorder,* in 1901 quoted the goal of the San Francisco Bar Association:

> The first and permanent aim to be obtained is the restoration of the profession in this city and county to its former place of honor and to restore its lost prestige.[13]

In 1909, Curtis H. Lindley, a professor at Boalt Hall and the first President of the California Bar Association, was quoted during his first term in office with respect to "two matters which received special attention":

> The first was the quality of the judiciary, and the second was to create in the public mind a respect for and confidence in the bench and bar.[14]

In reference to lawyers practicing in San Francisco during 1910, a report was submitted by Charles S. Wheeler, Chairman of the Ethics Committee, to the President and Members of the San Francisco Bar Association:

> In order to rehabilitate itself in the people's esteem, it must wake up and exact of itself the performance of its ethical obligations, a failure to do so would be a confession that it is, as a profession, unequal to the honorable duties which a patriotic people had laid upon it.[15]

In 1922, the Reverend John A. Wade, Chaplain of the New York Police Department, formerly of the Tombs, said:

> There is a stigma on the profession of lawyers as a result of the state of things which obtains in our criminal courts which it is for the profession to remove.[16]

In short, during and after the Progressive Era, the legal

profession was preoccupied with combatting the negative social images and public criticism stemming from their client-
oriented, public-blinded, and mercenary practices; and more
importantly, criticism was directed toward the bar's involvement in scandalous affairs within the administration of
justice (e.g., Eric Railroad Litigation, Tweed Frauds).

One of the principal arguments for public defenders concerned the potential elevation of the profession through the
elimination of "shysters" practicing in the criminal courts.
That many legal reforms were motivated by "interests," is
supported by an article written in 1916 by the Honorable
Milton Strasburger, "The Lawyer's Attitude Toward Social
Justice." Strasburger criticizes fellow lawyers and judges for
their lack of social consciousness and participation in matters of common welfare:

> Undoubtedly, some of the bar associations of the larger cities have
> brought about improvement in legal education and certain reforms
> in procedure and practice, etc.; but have the *contributions of these
> organizations to the relief of social conditions been as great as the
> situation demands*—assuming that we are responsible, in part, for
> such conditions?[17]

Later in the same article Strasburger contends that:

> Important reforms, admittedly feasible, are advocated from time to
> time by the leaders of our profession, but no concerted effort is
> made to cause the enactment of laws to bring about much reform.
> Are we indifferent to these matters concerning the common wel-
> fare, or are our own bar associations too conservative to consider
> questions of reform?[18]

Strasburger finishes his indictment of the legal profession by
pointing to the conspicuous absence of lawyers and judges
advocating or enacting important federal and state laws for
the purpose of improving social and economic conditions in
America. For example, Strasburger notes that the passage of
child labor laws, workmen's compensation, and safety com-
pliance acts were without the active support of the legal
profession.

Turning specifically to the issue of reforms advocated

within the system of criminal justice during and after the Progressive Era, the ideologies of monopoly capitalism and liberal reformism emerged as the dominant platform subscribed to by legal reformers. For example, in 1932, Professor Raymond Moley argued in the "New York Commission on Administration of Justice" that remedies within the criminal justice system would result from the incorporation of business methods into the various channels of the CJS, and from the increased cooperation between the bench and bar in an effort to pass legislation conducive to increased efficiency and economy.[19] A second example appears in an editorial, "Our Failure of Criminal Justice" in the *Journal of American Judicature Society* (1922). The author maintained that improvements in the fight against crime would result from the removal of politics from the courts; the upgrading of the legal profession; the administering of harsher sentences and more convictions; and the increased efficiency and decreased expense through a cooperative and unified criminal justice system.[20] In an editorial, "What's the Matter with the Courts? A Diagnosis," the editor of the *Journal of American Judicature Society* (1924) called for the modernization of the nineteenth-century court structure and procedure to accommodate the demands of the twentieth century; he also demanded the application of business principles to time-consuming court procedures (i.e., the dilatory tactics of defense lawyers), and the supervision of criminal procedure by a Judicial Council equal in strength to the legislature.[21] Finally, in an article entitled, "The Economic Basis for a Society of Advocates in the City of Chicago," Albert M. Kales, professor of law at Northwestern University, explained that the specialization and coordination of varied tasks, similar to the applied principles of elementary business, would result in a more economical and efficient administration of justice.[22]

The following quotes dramatize the preoccupation of legal reformers with business practices that were geared toward efficiency via cooperation, coordination, and centralization:

This is the age of business; practical men of affairs are in demand in all callings; theorists of scholarly tendencies but devoid of business acumen are not wanted.[23]

The hurry of business requires speedy results. Labor saving methods are demanded so that busy practitioners can economize their time.[24]

The most efficient means to expedition and thoroughness in the court is the centering in one head of the powers and general superintendence of the business of that court.[25]

. . . the duties of the judicial office . . . can be directed toward increased *efficiency in the administration of justice* and this, after all, is the only justifiable reform, change, modification or revolution which we ought to take with the courts.[26]

[Appellate Courts spend over fifty percent of their time in civil matters] ascertaining whether the machinery of the courts had been used in the exact technical manner prescribed by Congress and the legislatures. [That is to say, over 50% spent evaluating questions of "procedure" rather than on the "merits" of the case.] Could any business concern succeed with such a ratio of useless expense, and can the businessmen of this country afford to rest any longer under this senseless and extravagant condition?[27]

Sheton, author of the above quote and member of the Virginia Bar, finished his article with the argument that the time had come for the law to become a science, and justice, an absolute quantity. He did not, however, mention how this was to be accomplished.

These same general problems and remedies of the criminal justice system have been graphically described in an article by William E. Mikell:

Crime is no longer a local proposition, it is a statewide problem, to be handled by the state itself under modern executive and judicial methods. Our system of officers, our criminal pleadings, our court proceedings are all antiquated, rusty, disjointed and ineffective. We should strip sheriffs and constables of all but civil functions, abolish the coroner, county jails, and the grand jury, establish a state police with complete statewide power, and under their discretion employ experts in all criminal lines, put in a state bureau of criminal identification at the state penitentiary and criminal records that mean something throughout the state, give the district attorney all the powers of the grand jury, make the attorney general the head of the state law enforcement machinery, revise court procedure, put the state on an equality with the defendant [one of the arguments for the PDS (Public Defender System)], and make the court amount to something, so that we may have real judges, instead of umpires, sitting upon the bench.

This is a rather large dose for one taking, but the subject must be treated as a whole, and only by the most radical methods can we escape the truism uttered by Chief Justice Ţaft, "the administration of criminal law in America is a disgrace to civilization."[28]

Cantor, in *Crime: Criminals and Criminal Justice* (1932), also found the administration of justice to be impossibly complicated:

The American prosecutor cannot be asked to assume entire responsibility for the inefficient administration of criminal justice. That office is only part of the administrative machinery. The codes of criminal procedure regulating the conduct of the whole administrative process from arrest to sentence, the constitutional safeguards guaranteed every individual, such as the privilege against self-incrimination, and the right of the accused to be confronted with witnesses, freedom from unreasonable search and seizure, the operation of procedural rules no longer applicable to modern conditions, such as the requirements of the technical indictment, and the volume of work to which modern law enforcement had given rise—all present obstacles beyond the control of the prosecutor.[29]

Finally, the same theme of expediency, efficiency, and economy applies to the issue of the public defender. In an article, "In Defense of the Public Defender" (1917), the author argued that a division of labor in all fields is the natural product of an industrialized and urbanized society. With respect to criminal trials, the public defender becomes the logical complement of the district attorney, a situation conducive to cooperation, as opposed to the antagonism of the Assigned Counsel System (ACS), and a means consistent with the all-important goals of efficiency and economy.[30] In another article, "The Public Defender: The Complement of the District Attorney," Robert Ferrari* argued in 1912 that

---

* Robert Ferrari, as we will see later, was a principal advocate for the PDS, writing several essays favoring its development.

the public defender would improve criminal procedure; that
the PDS was the natural product of twentieth century bureaucracy; and that, as a dual agent of the client and the
state, the PDS would increase cooperation with the district
attorney. In other words, the PDS would contribute to a
more humane, economical, and efficient criminal prosecution.[31] In "The Necessity For A Public Defender," by
Mayer Goldman,* the argument was made that the public
defender is the most practical and economical solution to
the problems of criminal adjudication, especially with respect to eliminating the numerous reversals by appellate tribunals of convictions upon unfair trials.[32] And, in "Needed
Reforms in Criminal Law and Procedure," the author maintained that the public defender would reduce the competition between the two adversaries, thus reducing the fre-
quency and duration of delays in criminal proceedings.[33]

Pragmatism and Reformism

The corporate spirit of pragmatism and the bureaucratic
spirit of reformism merged to form an alliance against an
archaic system of laissez-faire criminal justice and the
counter-capitalist movements of the period. The ideology of
liberal reformism was legitimized by the social sciences, but
was borrowed and incorporated into the ideologies and phi-
losophies of businessmen, academicians, and legal professionals. Although separated by special interests (business
wanting to stabilize and control the political economy; aca-
demia wanting to elevate its status and marketability in the
field of applied sciences; and law wanting to elevate both
status and income while making the work of the adjudicative agents, as well as those of business, cheaper and simpler), all three groups were in general agreement whenever
issues of the status quo were at stake. In 1978 that bond still
exists under the guises of liberalism, behaviorism, and social

---

* Mayer Goldman was another principal advocate for the creation of public defender systems. In 1917, he wrote the first book on the subject, *The Public
Defender—A Necessary Factor in the Administration of Justice.*

engineering; it is particularly evident in the field of crime control under the rhetoric of "systems analysis," the "deterrence ideal," and "community-based" programs of intervention. Both during the Progressive Era and after, criminal justice reforms have been consonant with reforms in other social service institutions (e.g., education, health, welfare) in American society. That is to say, social policy, including reforms within the criminal justice system, has developed and been implemented in accommodative and ameliorative dosages designed to reinforce and maintain the existing social order and power relationships that are characteristic of American capitalism.

The ideas of cooperation, gradualism, and control spread rapidly throughout the organized bar. Members of the legal profession, representatives of the administration of criminal justice, and legal scholars argued for and against the different methods of representing accused indigents. Abstractly, the arguments focused on the outcomes of the criminal law. Issues revolved around the nature of the criminal lawyer in an adversary system; the conviction of the guilty and the acquittal of the innocent; the equality of justice before the law, regardless of social or class position; and lastly, the all-important status, or legitimacy, of both the law and legal profession.

The acceptance and ultimate approval of the public defender idea did not materialize until pragmatic justifications appeared for its institutionalization. The PDS did not emerge through the persuasions of the sincere and benevolent legal reformers who espoused the notions of "due process" and "social justice" for the poor as well as the rich. These arguments were not enough to convince the legal profession to support public defender bills in state legislatures. Between 1896 and 1914, year after year, bills were defeated across the country. However, after 1914, with the aid of examples such as Los Angeles and Portland, public defender bills were gradually enacted into law. *Not until reformers within the public defender movement could demonstrate an increased efficiency, a decreased expense, and a relative effectiveness compared to the ACS, was the PDS adopted.* Furthermore, the ideology of liberal reformism had to be employed in the language of legal reformers favoring the public defender. Thus, the public defender idea was celebrated as a reform within the administration of criminal justice that incorporated the various principles of modernization such as centralization, specialization, and coordination. Lastly, early fear of the PDS as being the first step towards a socialized bar had to be repudiated.

It must also be remembered that if reformers were sincerely interested in changing the existing economic, political, and social conditions responsible for the gross inequities within the law and society, they would have been as critical and reform-oriented toward injustice within the civil law as they were toward the injustice within the criminal law and the unethical practices of accusatorial justice. However, the development of an equitable civil law, with respect to the "class" position and individualized rights of the poor, was not at issue.[34] As Williams wrote of progressive reformers in general:

> When it came down to cases, they were unwilling to tamper with the anchor of the system—the legal interpenetration of the rights of private property and the corporation form of organization—for fear of damaging the former in weakening the latter.[35]

Hence, while most reformers were actively engaged in political reform, legal reformers kept to their own domain and concentrated on criminal law reforms. Thus change could only, at best, alleviate some symptoms and cover up others; but no fundamental alteration of the law or the political economy was regarded as necessary. The basic causes of inequities for the poor were ignored:

> For while their reforms were certainly understandable and defensible, and not wholly ineffective, they did not cut into the power structure of the corporation system. Strong on criticism and on proposals to strengthen their particular interests, the reformers were weak on ideas appropriate to the entire political economy.[36]

Finally, the contradictions and conflicts between vested interests and criminal justice reforms were succinctly articulated in "A Layman Looks at Justice." In that article, written in 1933, I. P. Gallison argued that:

> The preponderating cause of the failure of American justice is the American lawyer.... Any system so constructed that improvement and symmetrical growth are inimical to the material welfare of its personnel is fundamentally unsound. Alone among industrial and business enterprises and the "learned" professions, reform inevitably reacts to the material injury of the legal profession. Every proposal of value means loss of income, loss of power, and loss of position to the lawyer. Simply stated, the lawyer cannot reform the system nor permit others to reform it and survive.[37]

Defense Systems for the Poor: Assigned, Public, and Voluntary

All discussions involving the general topics of court reorganization, procedural reform, and improvement within the adjudicative processes were grounded in three beliefs concerning the breakdown and dissatisfaction with the administration of criminal justice. These were the abundance of delays in criminal prosecutions, the rising court costs, and the strategic positioning of the defense counsel for the indigent defendant and the associated expenses for litigation.[38] William Willoughby, in *Principles of Judicial Administration* (1929), described four methods for meeting the expense of litigation, especially for the indigent accused of violating the criminal law:

> (1) Elimination, as far as possible, of the need for counsel; (2) assignment by a court of counsel to act without compensation or for such compensation as the litigant may voluntarily offer; (3) provision by the government of counsel to care for the interests of those unable to meet the expense of employing private counsel; and (4) provision of counsel by private organizations specially created to render this service.[39]

The latter three methods emerged as defense systems for the poor. They were the Assigned Counsel System (ACS), the Public Defender System (PDS), and the Voluntary Defender System (VDS).

The Assigned Counsel System (ACS)

The ACS was the minimal machinery provided by laissez-faire criminal justice for processing the indigent offender:

'Under the ancient common law, persons accused of treason or felony were not permitted to defense, under the plea of not guilty, by counsel. The practice was not to permit counsel to be heard on questions of fact, but the court would assign counsel to be heard on questions of law arising on or after the trial. In such cases the prisoner proposed the point, and if the court supposed it would bear discussion, it assigned him counsel to argue it. (2 Hawkins' Pleas of the Crown, Chapter 39, section 4, p. 555, 1 Chitty on Criminal Law, 407.) Thus it appears that at the common law the court exercises the power of assigning counsel to argue legal questions, and it seems that counsel could only appear for the purpose after being assigned by the court. (*Johnson et al.* v. *Whiteside County,* 110 Illinois 22, 23.)'[40]

In the United States the sixth amendment to the Constitution guarantees the right to counsel. The various states reflected that right in their articles and cases as well as in their criminal codes throughout the 1800's and the first three decades of the 1900's. In the period preceding *Powell* v. *Alabama* (1932), a general pattern developed in metropolitan areas for the assignment of counsel for those defendants unable to procure counsel. In the majority of the states the law provided that the court, either on the request of the indigent or at its own discretion, was to appoint counsel. But as late as 1936, assignment was compulsory in only seven states; assignment was upon request in thirty states; and assignment was left to the court's discretion in nine states. Fees, if they were provided at all, were inadequate (with the exception of the places where capital cases were compensated). Thirteen states provided remunerations for misdemeanors, felonies, and capital crimes; five states, for only felony and capital offenses; eight states, for just capital cases. The inadequate fees allotted to the most exploited group within the legal profession, assigned counsels, contributed to the desperate conditions that these criminal lawyers found themselves in. Accordingly, Smith wrote in 1919 that:

The [assigned counsels] have procured fees in devious ways, ranging from compelling the mortgage to some share of all the household goods to forcing the prisoner's wife to sell herself on the street. That this degradation exists in connection with the administration of criminal justice is common knowledge.[41]

Moreover, in *Growth of Legal-Aid Work in the United States,* Smith and Bradway write:

This is a substantial defect in the assigned-counsel plan. It means that either the attorney must pay the incidental expenses out of his own pocket, which, of course, he cannot afford to do, and therefore does not do, or the defendant must go to trial and do the best he can in spite of an inadequate preparation of his cases.[42]

Counsel was most commonly chosen on a random or a rotating basis. In practice, however, the presiding judges' tendencies were to appoint counsel who were either young and inexperienced or old and without successful practices. Consequently, the most prominent and competent lawyers (usually in the fields of civil or corporate law) were ignored in the appointment process, as judges were well aware of the inconveniences caused to their practices. As Sutherland wrote of the ACS, "it is only in murder cases, in general, that competent and honest lawyers are willing to take assigned cases."[43]

Another weakness fundamental to most assignment systems was the late point at which counsel would intervene for the defendant. For example, only two states appointed counsel before the indictment; ten, before arraignment; fourteen, at the arraignment; and one, at the trial. Despite the lateness of assignment, the least competent counsel, the inadequate fee compensation, and the other inherent defects of the ACS, the system worked relatively well, at least to the satisfaction of the judicial agents and experts, in the laissez-faire society of nineteenth-century America. While the criminal justice system operated in a basically homogeneous population in small rural communities, there were relatively few criminal trials; hence, as appointments remained infrequent, there was little strain placed on attorneys. However, near the turn of the century, with the expanding population and growing urbanization, frequent appearances of "shyster" lawyers placed an economic burden on the judicial process, while denigrating the reputation of the legal profession as a whole. The situation was exacerbated throughout the nineties and into the Progressive Era. The number of cases requiring the assignment of attorneys expanded at a rate that was disproportionate with the number of available lawyers.[44] Finally, the inefficacy of the ACS had grown into a public issue; out of necessity and embarrassment, the conservative legal profession was forced to respond. Criticisms of the ACS, as well as of the administration of the criminal law, began appearing in newspapers, journals, law reviews, and governmental studies. The legal reformers' criticisms focused on the personnel, the inefficiency, and the expense of the ACS.

The personnel associated with the ACS were described by Brown as follows:

> Service is often rendered by attorneys who have just entered the profession and hence may not have the requisite experience. What is even more serious, it is often provided by 'jail lawyers,' 'shysters' or 'ambulance chasers'—men who have succeeded, 'by intimidation, threats, extortion, and even worse, in putting the assignment system on a commercial basis.' They are generally attorneys of small practice who, because of poor legal preparation or insufficient practice of an ethical nature, have been forced to utilize the unethical methods of 'professional' assigned counsel. No comment is necessary about a system of justice which permits such a situation to exist. When experienced attorneys are assigned to cases, they are inclined to neglect the poor for clients whose work is more remunerative.[45]

However, as mentioned previously, with the exception of an occasional murder case, successful attorneys with remunerative practices were unwilling to sacrifice the time and the money to defend poor people. The *New York Times,* on September 22, 1896, carried an article entitled, "Some Views of an Inferior Criminal Court." In the article, the types of counsel available under the ACS were characterized as "predatory," "hungry," and "occasional."[46] And Smith wrote that "back of the professional assigned counsel have grown up runners and straw bondsmen, who have worked their way into jails, corrupted officials and preyed on the prisoners."[47]

As early as the 1890's, the ACS was criticized for costing the court unnecessary delay and expense. Clara Foltz, one of the earliest advocates of the PDS, attributed the inadequacies to the fact that counsel was involved without a moment's notice, compelled to go to court without time to study the legal issues or to secure testimony, and to the fact that the pauper prisoners were usually forced to plead guilty for a lighter sentence so that the court saved valuable time and money.[48] Sutherland wrote that

> the poor defendant with an assigned counsel generally does not secure adequate protection; his lawyer is not efficient or is not interested, or uses this case merely as a means of extortion from defendant or his friends and relatives.[49]

Robert Ferrari explained that counsel for the poor was typically

> uncultivated, uneducated, rustic, boorish to the last degree and withal ignorant of the true principles of the criminal law. He is skilled only in tricks, in subterfuges, in meaningless and pointless objections, in tactics of obstruction.[50]

And Smith maintained that:

> The assignment of counsel in criminal cases, except when the offense charged is murder, has been a general failure. As a system, both in plan and operation, it deserves unqualified condemnation.

> In a word, the [murder] cases appeal simultaneously to the lawyer's self-interest and to the best traditions of his profession. The situation is reversed in other cases. The prisoner arrested for burglary, rape, or assault may arouse no sympathy, in fact the matter may be revolting.[51]

Nevertheless, Smith argued that even in the adequately

compensated cases of murder, assigned counsel undertakes a stance that knows no boundaries of honesty or propriety, a fact that often forces district attorneys out of impartial positions and into attitudes of hostility and distrust.

More specific criticisms of the assigned counsel system were directed at the following: (1) women posing as "Angels of Mercy" and advising the indigents to hire unscrupulous attorneys; (2) too many delays and inordinate use of continuances and technicalities; (3) too many jury trials and too many appeals; (4) too many cases left without counsel; (5) no cooperation or uniformity in trial procedure; (6) great expense of operation; (7) miscarriages of justice that revealed the disparities between the rich and the poor; and (8) adverse publicity subsequently directed against the legal profession as a whole.[52]

The Public Defender System (PDS)

In the early 1890's the public defender system was introduced as an alternative to the failing ACS. The idea of a public defender is actually quite old. Such a system existed in ancient Rome. Later, the Ecclesiastical Courts of the Middle Ages provided an office of advocate for the poor and an office of the procurator of charity. Both offices were regarded as highly honorable positions, as these courts recognized the needs of accused persons in matters of legal representation. Spain, as early as the fifteenth century, had an officer corresponding to a public defender. And in 1889 Belgium began a policy of public defense. By the turn of the twentieth century, the laws of the following countries provided an office of defenders: Argentina, Belgium, Denmark, England, France, Germany, Hungary, and Mexico.

In the United States, the idea dates back to the end of the eighteenth century. At the time of the Constitutional Conventions, which resulted in the first step taken to place the accused in a more favorable position in the eyes of the law, Benjamin Austin wrote:

As we have an Attorney General who acts in behalf of the State, it is proposed that the Legislature appoint another person (with a fixed salary) as Advocate General for all persons arraigned in criminal prosecutions; whose business should be to appear in behalf of all persons indicted by the State's Attorney. [53]

The idea, however, remained dormant for the next one-hundred years. But in 1896, bills were introduced in twelve state legislatures to establish public defender offices. "The purpose of [the bills] was to remove or mitigate grave evils in our criminal jurisprudence."[54] Extreme pressure was applied by members of the legal profession against the bills, and in all twelve states the bills were defeated. Despite the poor showing in the legislatures, hundreds of commendatory letters flowed to the respective state capitals. Over two hundred newspapers carried stories of the proposed legislation; where editorials appeared either against or in favor of the public defender, the tabulations revealed the following distribution: 50% were in favor, 40% were against, and the remaining 10% were in favor of a cheaper solution.[55]

If 1896 is used as the year the public defender movement began, it took approximately eighteen years for the first office of the public defender to be established. In 1914, a PDS was initiated in the County of Los Angeles. By 1916 the movement and discussion of the public defender idea had spread into twenty-five states.*

The objectives of the PDS were to eliminate some of the faults of the ACS in particular and those of the machinery of criminal justice in general. Specifically, the PDS was to be directed toward reducing the expenses and the inefficiencies of the ACS. The design and organization of the PDS was to be consistent with and reflective of the modern systems emphasizing a division of labor; through specialization and cooperation, the public defender and the district attor-

---

* Those states included Arizona, California, Connecticut, Georgia, Idaho, Illinois, Indiana, Iowa, Kansas, Massachusetts, Minnesota, Missouri, Nebraska, New Jersey, New York, North Carolina, North Dakota, Ohio, Oregon, Pennsylvania, Tennessee, Texas, Utah, Virginia, and Washington.

ney were to eliminate the cumbersome technicalities, safeguards, and loopholes employed by private counsel in behalf of non-indigent defendants. The legal reformers were able to rationalize, by relying on notions of "absolute" justice and truth, the PDS's role of acquitting the innocent rather than the guilty. Such a rationalization was unfair to the indigent defendant on two counts: first, the moral abstractions of justice and truth did not apply equally to the defendant who could afford to retain his own private counsel; and second, the presumption of innocence until proven guilty was to be all but officially removed for the poor defendant.

The ACS was the measuring stick used to determine the success of the PDS. In other words, if the PDS compared favorably to the ACS, then it should be adopted by all highly populated cities. Even within this context, however, the PDS was amelioristic in origin, as the standards of comparison did not include the best possible alternative—the defense of private counsel. A minority argued that, theoretically, the PDS should apply to all persons, rich or poor, accused of committing a crime. Moreover, the eventual abolishment of the private bar might have been in order:

> The time will come when, just as there has been an evolution from the private warfare of the past to the semicivilized administration of justice of the present, the private Bar will be abolished, as the private physician is almost abolished in England today. The profession will not be injured; it will be elevated, and benefited. But even if it would be injured, the community interests are primary.[56]

In fact, the Socialist National Platform of 1912 called for a socialized bar. However, the majority of the members of the legal profession feared the possibility of a completely socialized bar. It was not until after the fears surrounding the socialization of the bar were removed that the acceptance of the public defender by the American legal profession occurred. While the threat of a socialized bar was still alive, all bills for the creation of the office of public defender were defeated, except in Los Angeles. Even advocates of a socialized bar explained that, "for the time being," practicality and necessity require a PDS only where intolerable judicial conditions exist. Yet, what was ironic about this attitude was that intolerable judicial conditions were widespread; that they existed in large metropolitan cities where there were dense populations, heterogeneous in content, with a large number of poor and unemployed.

Another objective of the PDS was to provide secure legal jobs. The argument was made that economic pressures were forcing the less successful lawyers out of the corporate law, and with room for only some in general civil practices, many lawyers had to seek alternative non-professional occupations. Thus, the PDS was able to provide an alternative for some of these lawyers.

The PDS was also to lead the way toward other reforms within the administration of the criminal law and in the fight against crime. For example, the institutionalization of the PDS across the United States was supposed to permit the abolishment of the following constitutional guarantees: (1) the presumption of innocence; (2) the requirement of unanimous verdicts among jurors for a conviction; (3) the fifth amendment; and (4) the "hand-cuffing" rules of evidence. The argument was that these safeguards, originally needed to protect the accused from the state, could be eliminated because the public defender would be protection enough.[57]

With respect to the idealized goals of the PDS, some lawyers who were sincerely against the change from "private" to "public" defense contended that since the public defender system was to be quasi-judicial, lawyers for the poor defendant would not admit evidence they believed to be false, cross-examine witnesses if they believed their clients were guilty, nor would they demand jury trials to placate their clients. Instead, public defenders would encourage their clients to plead guilty; a quasi-inquisitorial system for the poor would be established; and lastly, under a PDS, the spirit of advocacy would be neglected.[58]

The following quotations represent arguments in favor of the public defender:

> The defender idea, in last analysis, is nothing more revolutionary than a plea for the extension of what is best in the assignment system and for reorganization along modern lines of efficiency.... As centralization of work makes for economy, efficiency, and responsibility, let there be, instead of a shifting group of attorneys, one definite official or organization charged with the duty of defending the poor, to whom all assignments may be made.[59]

> In favor of defenders was the belief that their offices would be more economical than the paying of fees to individual attorneys; they would provide, in general, better defense than the usual assigned counsel; the defendant would be assured of good preparation both in the law and in the facts of the case; a distinct savings of time would result; there would be a tendency to sift the deserving cases from the undeserving; they would aid the indigent defendant in obtaining a minimum sentence by entering a plea of guilty when such a plea was justified; fewer unscrupulous and perjured defenses would be attempted in court; the general tone of the criminal courts would be raised.[60]

> The defense of the accused under a public defender law would require no more time nor effort than is now consumed. Indeed, quite the contrary, for orderly arrangement of causes for trials would be far better effected between opposing offices than between a district attorney and a dozen lawyers with conflicting business.[61]

> He [the public defender] is supposed to expedite the trial of criminal cases ... reflected by the statutory services imposed on such an office ... by helping to eliminate all those where there is no need for a trial and by sorting out the cases where the person is clearly not guilty, thus saving the county the expense of complicated proceedings.[62]

> The proper duty of the prosecuting attorney is not to secure a conviction, but to convict only after a fair and impartial trial. Upon the same principle it is not the duty of the public defender to secure acquittals of guilty persons, but to endeavor to ascertain the true facts and to go to trial upon these facts, the aim of both officials would be to go to work in harmony to bring out a just administration of the law.[63]

> He should cooperate with the district attorney, whenever not inconsistent with his client, and whenever possible, in order to bring

about an ideal administration of the law. His duty should be to protect the innocent—not to acquit the guilty.[64]

This office would, in co-operation with the probation staff, be of material assistance in securing that information which the court needs to arrive at a just sentence. Finally, such an organization, through its constant contact with the criminal work of the court and through its reports, would be the sort of guardian and watcher which is essential if the public is to be kept intelligently informed of what goes on in its legal institutions.[65]

Ideally, the duties of the public defender, as defined in 1913, were:

[The public defender] (a) shall defend without expense any defendant unable financially and charged with commission of any content or offense triable in the Superior Court, including all stages of prosecution and appeal where indicated, (b) shall prosecute actions for collection of wages, (c) shall, upon request, defend any person unable financially in any civil litigation. (Government Code 27700–27711, Section 27706.)[66]

The manner in which the public defender office was to operate is as such: first, the indigent defendant without the aid of counsel was referred to the public defender office. At that point, the meeting of the public defender and the accused took place at the jail, and the case for the defense was initiated by investigation.* When the investigation was completed, the public defender

advis[ed] the defendant as to his rights under the law, and further advis[ed] him as to what his plea should be —guilty or not guilty— whether it [was] better to have a jury trial or waiver thereof and [apply] for probation . . . .[67]

By design, the public defender was to provide a defense which was equal to or better than the ACS:

---

* As early as 1919, it was recognized that the public defender rarely prepared his defense beyond the obvious merits of the case. In other words, unlike the privately retained criminal lawyer, the public defender lacked "incentive for doing anything beyond what was ethically proper." (See Reginald Smith, *Justice and the Poor,* The Carnegie Foundation for the Advancement of Teaching, Bulletin 13 (New York City: 1919), p. 84.)

It cannot be proved that the defender plan affords better protection to innocent defendants than the assigned-counsel plan. It is the belief of the writers of this report, however, that the defender plan serves the defendant as well as the paid assigned-counsel plan. And that it is inherently a *more efficient and more economical method of getting the necessary work done.*[68] (Emphasis added)

Not surprisingly, the PDS was not, as mentioned earlier, first evaluated in comparison with the work of private attorneys to determine whether the office should spread across the country. When using, for example, the comparative statistics of acquittals, sentencing, and probation, categorically, the private defense counsel was superior to the public defender. However, with respect to the length of trial and costs to the court, the PDS offered a significant savings over the ACS or private counsel.[69]

With respect to a working-model, the PDS was described in an open letter by Henry L. Lyons, public defender of Portland, which appeared in the *San Francisco Recorder,* March 2, 1914:

As the work was new here there was some question as to how far the public defender should go, or how energetic he should be in the defense of those he represents. For that reason it was thought best . . . that the public defender should limit his defense to assisting court in bringing out the prisoner's side of the case, rather than making a vigorous fight on technical grounds necessary to secure an acquittal.[70]

And Smith and Bradway wrote:

We find the district attorney and the defense working harmoniously together on sincere cooperation for the advancement of justice. It is no accident that most of the defender organizations have been established at the instances of judges and lawyers familiar with the criminal law, and the best proof of the essential merit of the defender's work is that wherever it exists it is supported and commended by the district attorney's office and by the judges of the criminal courts.[71]

The above two passages reveal how, from the beginning, the PDS was to assist the court and complement the district attorney rather than provide a rigorous and adversarial defense for the accused. It is no surprise that on June 29, 1916, the inmates of Sing Sing in *The Mutual Welfare League Bulletin of Sing Sing Prison* came out against the public defender system and opposed the establishment of public defender offices.

By 1917, public defender bills had been introduced in twenty states. By 1920 there were five public defender offices; and by 1926 there were twelve. By 1933 at least twenty-one public defender offices had been started. Laws for the creation of a PDS had passed in the following states: California, Connecticut, Illinois, Indiana, Minnesota, Nebraska, Ohio, Tennessee, and Virginia. Other highly populated cities, including Pittsburgh, Philadelphia, New York City, Rochester, and Cleveland had adopted the VDS to combat the inadequacies of the ACS.

The Voluntary Defender System (VDS)

The second most desirable alternative to the ACS was the Voluntary Defender System (VDS). In highly populated cities (e.g., usually over 100,000 people) where the PDS was not selected, the chances were that a VDS was created. In 1917 the first private organization with the expressed purpose of defending the indigent accused of crimes was initiated by James B. Reynolds and a group of followers. The office was called the Voluntary Defenders Committee of New York and was created as the result of two events: first, the strong and determined opposition of the Bar Association of New York and the New York County Lawyers Association to the PDS; and second, the failure of the Wade Plan, an attempt by the New York Legal Aid Society to maintain a criminal branch.[72] If neither a PDS nor a successful legal-aid approach were to be established, then another alternative to the ACS had to be devised; and consequently, a "systematic provision for the defense of the indigent accused was made . . . ."[73]

Despite the distinction made between "private" and "public" defense, the VDS was patterned much like the PDS.

Structurally, both offices used the law office approach of the large law firms, complete with a conspicuous division of labor incorporating all the necessary resources and specialties required of investigations, trials, and appeals. The VDS, however, was to be a private, non-profit, and non-governmentally controlled agency. Financial contributions paying for the expense of the office and personnel were to come from private philanthropy. But it was not too long before the office had become dependent on government for approximately one-half of its budget. Furthermore, the office was located, free of rent, inside the Criminal Courts Building, and juxtaposed to the office of the district attorney.

The legal reformers in favor of the VDS rather than the PDS argued that there were two advantages to the former system: the office would remain within the private domain of the bar and the possibility of another public office becoming subject to political spoils and corruption would be eliminated.

The attorneys of the first VDS were derived from a list of counsel who were willing to advocate in trial but not willing to prepare the defense prior to trial. The list consisted of lawyers in private practice who had previously served with honor in the district attorney's office. Additional personnel within the office consisted of investigators, secretaries, and lawyer-apprentices who prepared the briefs. All members of the office received small salaries. Early financial backing for this office came from John D. Rockefeller, Jr.

With respect to a working-model, both the VDS and the PDS were essentially the same. The basic goals of each office were: (1) to seek the truth and not acquittals; (2) to maintain harmony and cooperation with the prosecution; and (3) to save both time and money. The following two quotes, the first by the Committee on Public Defenders, express the similarities between the PDS and the VDS:

> We felt that it was inconsistent with our social duty as high-minded, decent citizens to go in and take up the time of the court with cases where the defendant was apparently guilty.[74]

Mr. Barton [Prosecutor of New York City] has publicly appealed for funds to keep the Defenders going. Complete confidence prevails between the two. Frank discussions pro and con on pending cases are not uncommon, leading sometimes to prompt pleas of guilty, sometimes to the dropping of prosecutions. Even where such an interchange does not dispose of the controversy, court draws the issues more tightly, *making trial simpler, swifter, and cheaper.*[75] (Emphasis added)

And as Louis Fabricant, a lawyer with the Voluntary Defenders Committee of New York, pointed out, the objective of acquittal is often subordinated to the objective of fact finding:

When we start the defense of a man, it is not always a contest to establish his innocence—it is an endeavor to find the facts, . . . as a result of that type of investigation . . . , we find that it is not always true that innocent men are being sacrificed on the altar of the master "Injustice," that, in fact, many of these men are guilty.[76]

Arguments Surrounding the Creation of the Public Defender System

The arguments for and against the creation of the PDS accentuate the four interrelated themes of this work. That is, the institutionalization of the public defender, a reform within the administration of criminal justice, initiated by various groups directly or indirectly involved with the apparatus of crime control, represented, served and/or exemplified: (1) the amelioristic attempt to solve the problems of the unrepresented indigent caused by the deteriorating judicial process in metropolitan areas; (2) the vested interests of the legal profession, judicial agents, and the larger political economy; (3) the diffusing of the ideology of liberal reformism into the emerging fields of professional law enforcement and criminal justice management/administration; and (4) the rationalization, legitimation, and maintenance of the democratic ideals of due process and equal justice for all.

The arguments concerning the creation of the PDS centered on (1) questions of theory—whether or not the PDS could serve the purposes of law, and on (2) questions of practicality—whether or not the PDS could efficiently and economically expedite the criminal justice process. However, before summarizing the arguments surrounding the creation of the PDS, it should be pointed out that neither those who favored nor those who opposed the public defender idea ever seriously challenged the rule of law concept of adversary justice. It should also be noted that those individuals or groups who have been involved in the various public defender debates over the past century have never seriously questioned the PDS and its relationship to the underlying political economy of crime control in capitalist society.

The arguments presented below are divided according to whether or not they appeared before or after 1914, the year the PDS was initiated. Before 1914, the arguments in favor of the PDS generally appealed to a rule of law concept that maintained that the proper role of the State should be to shield the innocent as well as convict the guilty. Relying on the "presumption of innocence" principle, advocates for the public defender reform argued that the State should provide two organizational offices—the D.A. and the PD—for the adjudication of criminal defendants, not just a district attorney's office with the dual responsiblilty of carrying out contradictory functions—prosecution and defense. In this way, procedural safeguards for the accused would be more closely adhered to, cases would be more honestly and evenly prosecuted, and by the fact that the State would remunerate attorneys for their services, the less scrupulous lawyers who prey on the poor would be eliminated. In short, the general tone of the criminal court would be raised, the status of the legal profession would be elevated, and "unfair discrimination" between the rich and the poor would be removed. Foltz's comments are characteristic of the arguments made by the early reformers who favored the public defender:

> In a country whose primary function and highest duty is to protect and defend its people one would expect to find courts provided with all the essentials of justice. But they are not. The prisoner is merely told that he may buy this essential and thus buy justice in a land that boasts that justice is free.[77]

The arrested man is not brought before an impartial tribunal for trial, but before one where legal skill, police venality, money reward, and oftimes popular effort is made to secure not justice but conviction.[78]

Court appointees do not come from the successful ranks of the profession. Once in awhile the court braves the resentment of a busy lawyer and appoints him. In practice appointees come from the loafers in court and from the young, the untried and inexperienced in the profession, without money, skill, or interest in the result.[79]

The State will not only perform its duty but will promote exact and equal justice, protect the poor, save the innocent and remove an unjust burden from a generous profession.[80]

Before 1914, the arguments against the PDS generally appealed to a rule of law concept which maintained that the proper role of the State should be neutral and objective, more distant and less costly. Otherwise, those opposed to the public defender idea, argued that the spirit of advocacy would be lost as defendants would be persuaded to plead guilty and waive their fundamental rights to jury trials. In short, the accusatory system would be replaced by an inquisitorial system which was not only costly to the State in economic terms, but which also provided the opportunities for creating another political office. At this time, there were also arguments which viewed the operation of two offices by the State as both contradictory and overlapping. After all, the appellate courts already existed for the purposes of correcting any wrongs done to criminal defendants. Finally, some opponents argued that the young and inexperienced lawyers would have no clients left to practice criminal law on, and that the institutionalization of the PDS could lead to a socialized bar. The following quotes are indicative of those individuals opposed to the public defender:

The defender would become so hardened to the stories of defendants that he might become indifferent to the justice of each case or he might become inclined to disbelieve their stories, he would not show the same degree of enthusiasm as would the attorney assigned to defend a particular case; as the result of indifference and lack of enthusiasm, he would be likely to recommend that pleas of "guilty" be entered; the office of defender would create another political position with the likelihood of accompanying patronage and corruption; many cases would be prosecuted and defended by the same group of men, because the prosecutor and defender would often act together.[81]

[The PDS would enable] poor people to secure legal assistance so that they can play the legal game more efficiently than at present. It tends to perpetuate the sporting element and the contentiousness of the courts.[82]

One group of objections is based on the belief that the defender is a person whose duty is to keep dishonest persons from going to jail. It is contended that such a person will frustrate the efforts of the district attorney; that the State should not champion criminals; that it is illogical to have one official to put men in jail and another to keep them out.[83]

Another group of objections alleges that the defender is superfluous. It is argued that the laws throw safeguards around the person of the accused; that the judge and the district attorney are bound to protect him.[84]

The arguments after 1914 were based primarily on the practical experiences and statistics of the PDS in Los Angeles. The significant changes in the arguments were: first, those favoring the creation became almost totally dependent on efficiency, economy, and effectiveness, with only a small amount of rhetoric paid to the issues of social justice, competency of counsel, and the rights of the accused; and second, those against the PDS maintained the same arguments excluding the contention of increased cost, political corruption, and a socialized bar.

Advocates for the public defender maintained that compared to the Assigned Council System, there were fewer delays, fewer trials with and without juries, and a more efficient processing of criminal defendants due to both a reduction in the use of procedural technicalities and to the centralization and specialization of the public defender's office. Moreover, the increased cooperation and harmony between the district attorney's office and the public defender's office had resulted in more guilty pleas and quicker selection of juries when trials were necessary, thus helping to alleviate the backlog and congestion of overcrowded court dockets. The following are quotations of arguments favoring the public defender:

'The assigned counsel system should give way to the more modern, more efficient, more economical public defender system. The greater success attending the assignment of all cases of all accused poor persons to one central responsible agency has been demonstrated in Los Angeles.'[85]

District attorneys from their position might be expected to be hostile, but in fact have been the warmest endorsers of the work and the chairman knows of no prosecuting attorney who had dealt with a public defender who does not approve the work.[86]

Except for cases of great magnitude, practice in the criminal courts had mostly fallen into the hands of the lower stratum, with the result, among others, that the common-law mitigating agencies, meant to be checks, have come to require checks and are in effect without any.[87]

[The public defender] does not have conflicting engagements, does not need to secure continuances, does not make formal motions for the purpose of delay and makes fewer appeals to higher courts.[88]

'It is the general opinion of the judges of this district that the system had not only proven practicable but has the approval of all of the judges that it has been successful. The former system of appointing attorneys for the defense of penurious defendants was more expensive than the present method which operates with less inconvenience to the court and with fully as great a protection to the defendants.'[89]

The problem arises when a multitude of poor persons, unable to pay a fee, becomes so great that the individual lawyer cannot afford to give more time to them. In the modern law office there is a definite limit to the amount of aid of this sort which can be given.[90]

It is probably not inaccurate to estimate that to secure adequate representation for indigent prisoners by paying assigned counsel is twice as expensive as by the defender plan.[91]

The criticisms or arguments against the PDS after 1914 were not very loud or strong. In short, they revolved around two issues: (1) the loss or decline in the adversary system brought about by the close working proximity of judges, district attorneys, and public defenders; and (2) the expense, inefficiency, and burden created by the establishment of another civil service, governmental bureaucracy.

In conclusion, the arguments—pro and con—surrounding the creation of the PDS were preoccupied with the appropriate procedural remedies for administering the criminal law. Both at the time of the creation of the public defender and today the ends of the criminal justice system and the substantive content of the law have remained divorced from the "debate" on the PDS. And accordingly, the PDS has always been celebrated as a progressive reform, despite the fact that this reform has never served to benefit as a whole that group of legal offenders for which it was intended.

Once corporate lawyers were persuaded that the vested interests of the legal profession were not threatened by the PDS, the PDS was accepted as a viable reform consistent with the needs of the growing socio-economic order. The PDS adapted itself perfectly to a Progressivism that was:

> [a] mild and judicious movement, whose goal was not a sharp change in the social structure, but rather the formation of a responsible elite (corporate lawyers), which was to take charge of the popular impulse toward change and direct it into modern and, as they would have said, "constructive" channels.[92]

Moreover, the formation of the PDS was consistent with the emerging principles of a modern division of labor, of technocracy, and of corporate liberalism generally. Therefore, whether the arguments favoring the institutionalization of the PDS emphasized due process and equal protection under the law, or economy and efficiency, the result was that the PDS served the needs of the growing corporate order and not the ideals of social justice.

Finally, the basic inequities inherent in the class-specific legal order were strengthened by the creation of the PDS. The PDS actually deprived the poor of the careful and dedicated legal representation they desperately needed. In the meantime, private defense remained a luxury for those who could afford it. Consequently, the stage was set whereby legal representation for the poor would no longer be the activity and problem of the private bar, but would instead become the object of governmental control and regulation.

NOTES

1. Quoted in William Appleman Williams, *The Contours of American History,* (Chicago: Quadrangle, 1966), p. 371.
2. See for examples, Lester Ward, *Dynamic Sociology,* (New York: D. Appleton & Co., 1883), 2 vols.; Edward A. Ross, *Foundations of Somatism,* (New York: Longmans, Green and Co., 1907); and John Dewey, "Evolution and Ethics," *Monist,* VIII (1898), pp. 321–341.
3. Samuel Mencher, *Poor Law to Poverty Program,* (Pittsburgh: University of Pittsburgh Press, 1967), p. 266; see also, Eric F. Goldman, *Rendevous with Destiny: A History of Modern American Reform,* (New York: Random House, Inc., 1955). In addition, it should be noted that such legal scholars as Brandeis, Cardoza, and Pound were constantly making arguments that unless changes within the law, and especially the administration of the criminal law were made, social disorder would result.
4. Roscoe Pound, *An Introductory to the Philosophy of Law,* (New Haven: Yale University Press, 1922), p. 99.
5. Roscoe Pound, "Jurisprudence," in *Encyclopedia of Social Science,* vol. 8. p. 484, (1916).
6. Sheldon Glueck, "The Social Sciences and Scientific Method in the Administration of Justice," *The American Academy of Political and Social Science,* vol. 167, (May 1933), p. 110.
7. George W. Wickersham, "The American Law Institute," *University of Pennsylvania Law Review,* vol. 72, pp. 1–23.
8. Nathaniel F. Cantor, *Crime: Criminals and Criminal Justice,* (New York: Henry Holt and Co., 1932), p. 174.
9. For this and the second through fourth points, see the general works of Gabriel Kolko, James Weinstein, William A. Williams, and Ralph Miliband.
10. Williams, *Contours of American History,* p. 418.
11. Quoted in Williams, *Contours of American History,* p. 390.
12. "The Illinois Crime Survey," in the *Journal of Criminal Law and Criminology,* vol. 20, (1929–30), p. 599.
13. Quoted in *The Bar Association of San Francisco: The First Hundred Years (1872–1972),* by Kenneth M. Johnson, (Recorder Printing and Publishing Co., 1972), pp. 23–4.
14. Ibid., p. 39.
15. Ibid., pp. 44–45.

16. Quoted in John Maguire, *The Lance of Justice: A Semi-Centennial History of the Legal Aid Society (1876–1926),* (Cambridge: Harvard University Press, 1928), p. 266.

17. Milton Strasburger, "The Lawyer's Attitude Toward Social Justice," *Case and Comment,* vol. 23, (1916–1917), p. 978.

18. Ibid., p. 979.

19. Raymond Moley, "New York Commission on Administration of Justice," *The Panel,* (May–June 1932).

20. "Our Failure of Criminal Justice," *Journal of American Judicature Society,* (February 1922), vol. 5, no. 5.

21. "What's the Matter with the Courts? A Diagnosis," *Journal of American Judicature Society,* (February 1924), vol. 7, no. 5, pp. 151–55.

22. Albert M. Kales, "The Economic Basis for a Society of Advocates in the City of Chicago," *Illinois Law Review,* vol. 9, (1914–15).

23. George F. Shelton, "Law as Business," *Yale Law Journal,* vol. 10, p. 275., (1900–01).

24. Ibid., p. 276.

25. T. Kent Greene, "The Municipal Court of Chicago, *University of Pennsylvania Law Review,* vol. 58 (1909–1910), p. 343.

26. Howard A. Lehman, "Some Practical Remedies For Existing Defects in the Administration of Justice," *University of Pennsylvania Law Review,* vol. 61 (1912–13), p. 20.

27. Thomas W. Sheton, "An Efficient Judicial System," *Case and Comment,* vol. 22, (1915–16), p. 228.

28. Quoted in William E. Mikell, "Criminal Procedure—Defects in its Administration," *The Annals of the American Academy of Political and Social Science,* vols. 125–26, (May–July 1926).

29. Cantor, *Crime: Criminals,* p. 189.

30. Abram E. Adelman, "In Defense of the Public Defender," *The Journal of Criminal Law and Criminology,* vol. 5, (November 1917), p. 494.

31. Robert Ferrari, "The Public Defender: The Compliment of the District Attorney," *Journal of Criminal Law and Criminology,* (January 1912).

32. Mayer Goldman, "The Necessity for a Public Defender," *The Journal of Criminal Law and Criminology,* (January 1915).

33. William Lawlor, "Needed Reforms in Criminal Law and Procedure," *Journal of Criminal Law and Criminology,* (March 1911).

34. Robert Lefcourt (ed.), *Law Against The People,* (New York: Vintage, 1966).

35. Williams, *Contours of American History,* pp. 396–7.

36. Ibid.

37. I. P. Gallison, "A Layman Looks at Justice," *Journal of the American Judicature Society,* vol. 16, (April 1933), pp. 176–181.

38. See generally, Reginald Heber Smith and John S. Bradway, *Growth of Legal-Aid Work in the United States,* Bulletin No. 607, (Washington: U.S. Government Printing Office, Department of Labor, 1936).

39. Quoted in ibid., p. 22.
40. Quoted in Charles Mishkin, "The Public Defender," *The American Journal of Criminal Law and Criminology,* vol. 22, (1931–32), p. 490.
41. Reginald Heber Smith, *Justice and the Poor,* The Carnegie Foundation for the Advancement of Teaching, Bulletin No. 13, (New York City: 1919), p. 114.
42. R. H. Smith and Bradway, *Growth of Legal Aid Work,* p. 78.
43. Edwin H. Sutherland, *Criminology,* (Philadelphia and London: J. B. Lippincott Co., fifth impression, 1924), p. 267.
44. See generally, Special Committee to Study Defender Systems' *Equal Justice for the Accused,* (New York: Doubleday & Co., 1959); Herman I. Pollock, "Equal Justice in Practice," *Minnesota Law Review,* vol. 45; Gerald Wayne Smith, *A Comparative Examination of the Public and Private Attorneys in a Major California County,* (U. C. Berkeley, School of Criminology, 1969); and Silverstein's *Defense of the Poor,* (Chicago: American Bar Foundation, 1965).
45. Esther Lucile Brown, *Lawyers and the Promotion of Justice,* (New York: Russel Sage Foundation, 1938), p. 254.
46. *New York Times,* (September 22, 1896).
47. Smith and Bradway, *Growth of Legal Aid Work,* p. 114.
48. Clara Foltz, "Public Defenders," 25 *Chicago Legal News,* (1893), p. 431.

49. Sutherland, *Criminology,* p. 268.
50. Robert Ferrari, "The Public Defender," p. 706.
51. R. H. Smith, *Justice and the Poor,* pp. 114 and 112 respectfully.
52. See generally, articles by Foltz, R. H. Smith, Ferrari, and Mishkin.
53. Quoted in Smith and Bradway, *Growth of Legal Aid Work,* pp. 115–16.
54. Clara Foltz, "The Public Defender," *American Law Review,* (1897 May–June), vol. 31, p. 393.
55. Ibid., pp. 395–96.
56. Robert Ferrari, "An Argument For the Public Defender," *Journal of American Institute of Criminal Law and Criminology,* (March 1915), vol. 5, p. 927.
57. See generally, ibid.
58. See generally, Foltz, "The Public Defender," (1897).
59. R. H. Smith, *Justice and the Poor,* p. 116.
60. Brown, *Lawyers,* p. 257.
61. Foltz, "The Public Defender," (1897), pp. 401–02.
62. R. H. Smith et al., *Growth of Legal Aid Work,* p. 79.

63. Samuel Rubin, "Criminal Justice and the Poor," *Journal of the American Institute of Criminal Law and Criminology,* vol. 22, (1931–32), p. 715.
64. M. Goldman, "The Necessity for a Public Defender," p. 8.
65. Quoted in Reginald H. Smith, "Defender in Criminal Cases Recommended in Cleveland," *Journal of Criminal Law and Criminology,* vol. 12, (1921–22).

66. The Public Defender Law of Los Angeles County (Government Code 27700–27711, Section 27706); with respect to points b and c, these duties have now become the work of legal-aid organizations.

67. *Report of the Judicial Advisory Council of Cook County,* (January 1931), p. 25.

68. *Report of the Judicial Advisory Council of Cook County,* (January 1931), p. 26.

69. See generally, Smith and Bradway, *Growth of Legal Aid Work;* Brown, *Lawyers;* and more specifically, Raymond Moley, "The Vanishing Jury," *Southern California Law Review,* vol. II, no. 2, (Dec., 1928).

70. *San Francisco Recorder,* (March 2, 1914).

71. R. H. Smith et al., *Growth of Legal Aid Work,* p. 95.

72. John Maguire, *The Lance of Justice,* p. 269.

73. Report on Prosecution, Wickersham Commission, *National Commission on Law Observance and Enforcement,* (Washington: U.S. Government Printing Office, 1931), p. 32.

74. James Reynolds, "The Public Defender," read at the 3rd annual meeting of the American Institute of Criminal Law and Criminology by the Committee on Public Defenders, p. 483 in the *Journal of American Institute of Criminal Law and Criminology,* vol. 12, (1921–22).

75. Maguire, *The Lance of Justice,* p. 277.

76. J. Reynolds, "The Public Defender," p. 487.

77. Foltz, "The Public Defender," p. 397.

78. Ibid.

79. Ibid., p. 399.

80. Ibid., p. 403.

81. Brown, *Lawyers,* pp. 257–58.

82. Sutherland, *Criminology,* p. 270.

83. Smith et al., *Growth of Legal Aid Work,* p. 73.

84. Ibid.

85. Quoted in R. H. Smith, *Justice and the Poor.*

86. J. Reynolds, "The Public Defender," p. 477.

87. Pound, *Philosophy of Law,* p. 195.

88. Quoted in Sutherland, *Criminology,* p. 268.

89. Quoted in "The Public Defender," *American Journal of Criminal Law and Criminology,* (1931–32), vol. 22, p. 500; (original from Grier M. Orr, Judge of the District Court of St. Paul).

90. Rubin, "Criminal Justice and the Poor," p. 711.

91. R. H. Smith, *Justice and the Poor,* p. 120.

92. Richard Hofstadter, *The Age of Reform: From Bryan to F.D.R.,* (New York: Random House, Inc., 1955), p. 163.

4 CRIME / CLASS CONTROL: Progression

During the period of transition from a laissez-faire to a monopolistic system of capitalism, the country was experiencing bitter class wars. The working classes aggressively resisted exploitation through on-the-job actions and wider social movements. Initially, the ruling classes employed unsanctioned violence, such as the hiring of thugs and private armies, to combat challenges to the emerging corporate order. However, as the number of violent incidences increased, and as the contradictions of American democracy became more apparent, other methods of controlling the masses (i.e., the formation of state police systems) were substituted. Armed with the ideologies of pragmatism and social responsibility, the progressive leaders and reformers were able to implement the practices of welfare, accommodations and assimilation.

With the combined promises of gradual reform and general prosperity and security, the ruling groups in America were able to override opposing social and philosophical critics of capitalism. In the process, the foundations for the modern system of crime control were laid and the legitimacy of the liberal democratic approach was ingrained in the American mentality. Ultimately, mass education, working-class citizenship, assimilation of ethnic groups, voting privileges, political parties, and economic mobility of the expanding middle class contributed to the stabilization of a society undergoing drastic changes.

Throughout the Progressive Era, the administration of criminal justice underwent major reorganization—the criminal justice system had to adapt to the needs of a modern corporate order.

Reform was necessary so that the capitalistic impetus could progress unimpeded by social disorder. Increased crime (class) control was necessary because, as Rubin states,

despite corporate capitalism's control of the state and its hegemony over the rest of society in the years between 1890 and 1920, this was a period of much fear and uncertainty for the business community.[1]

The plight of the poor gained the attention of the more powerful elements of society; the discontent of those who were not benefiting from the surge of corporate capitalism threatened the growing prosperity of those who were. As a response to the growing resentment of the lower classes, the more powerful elements of society sought to stabilize the social order. This was done, in conjunction with middle-class reform groups, by offering seemingly humane programs that would help to disguise the more obvious contradictions of the emerging corporate order.[2]

The many reform movements in criminal justice, of which the PDS, the juvenile justice system, and the indeterminate sentencing system are notable examples, sought to improve the more blatantly inhumane conditions of a laissez-faire system of crime control. Sentencing goals, such as deterrence, rehabilitation, and commensurate desert, were espoused as necessary to the public welfare.

Social Disorder in Progressive America

The last decade of the nineteenth century and the first two decades of the twentieth century were depicted by social, political, economic, and legal reformers as being chaotic, disruptive, and precarious for the future survival of monopoly capitalism. Abraham Epstein, a Roosevelt policymaker, stated early in the 1900's that the

insecurity of the wage earner endangers the very existence of the social order. No society that exposes the majority of its members to

such grave and continuous hazards and injustices can endure for
long.[3]

This period in American history is recognized for its economic depressions, rising prices, industrial conflicts, political
strife and corruption, social dissension, rapid urbanization,
influx of immigrants, and increasing poverty and criminality.[4]

By the turn of the century, the basis for renewed optimism on the part of the ordinary man, in the city as well as on
the farm, began to wane. Accountable for the skeptical outlook were the closing of the frontier, the dwindling supply of
cheap land, and the expanding control of the larger corporations over the use and exploitation of natural and human
resources. Moreover, prior to World War I, the changing political economy, the shifting nature of the population,* and
the shrinking possibilities of making a "legitimate" living
brought about a continuous cycle of industrial depressions:
1857–1858, 1873–1879, 1893–1897, 1907–1908, and 1913–1917.
By 1866 the United States was experiencing severe class conflict and struggle, epitomized by the Haymarket Riot of that
year. The conflict and dissension lasted throughout the Wilson administration. Included among the more scandalous in-
cidents were the Rochester Clothing Manufacturing Strike,
the Pullman and Homestead Strikes, the National Coal
Strike, the Goldfield and Tonopah (silver) Strikes, the Spokane Lumber Strike, the Wheatland Riot, the Ludlow Massacre, the Centralia Massacre, and the infamous Palmer
Raids. In addition, social movements and organizations (e.g.,
International Workers of the World; Bolsheviks; commun-
ists; socialists; and anarchists) opposed to and alien to the
"American way of doing things" were flourishing. For example, during this period the free speech movement of the
Wobblies was becoming contagious:

---

* In 1840, the U.S. population was estimated to be just over 17 million, of which 90%
was rural. In 1910, the population had climbed to approximately 92 million, of
which 50% was urban. Thus, in 70 years the general population increased almost
five and one-half times, and the urban population increased 27 times.

From Spokane in 1909 to San Diego in 1912, through Washington, Montana, South Dakota, Minnesota, Wisconsin, Pennsylvania, Massachusetts, Missouri, [Nevada] and Colorado, the I.W.W. inoculated otherwise peaceful communities with the virus of repression.[5]

What is more, the Socialist Party of 1912 was peaking in popularity, electing 1,039 socialists to various offices throughout the country. And, while losing his bid for the Presidency, Eugene Debs polled almost a million votes. His strong showing certainly revealed the potential threat of those who rejected the ethic of capitalism.[6]

What was happening in the state of California at the time of the creation of the earliest PDS? During the summer of 1913 the prosperity of the past few years had vanished, and industrial depression had settled in California, as it had in the rest of the country. Tensions between labor and capital were great. On August 3, 1913, the first major skirmish took place—the Wheatland Riot. At the Durst Hop Ranch, 2800 migratory workers led by Blackie Ford, with at least a score of members of the I.W.W., held a mass meeting to protest the wages and unsatisfactory working and sanitary conditions. George E. Mowry in *The California Progressives* described the incident:

Almost immediately, however, a sheriff's posse appeared. When the district attorney started toward the assembled workers to arrest Ford, a shot was fired. After a few minutes of confused struggle four men, including the district attorney, a deputy sheriff, and two workers, were dead. Many more were injured. Within hours, four companies of the National Guard were maintaining order over the surrounding countryside.[7]

Unemployment and breadlines were also increasing:

By the late fall of 1913 the [California] board of immigration estimated that 75,000 men were unemployed in San Francisco and Los Angeles alone. All through the dark winter breadlines and resentment grew, and in the spring the talk of an unemployed march on the national capital rapidly spread the length of the state.[8]

Later in the same year, urban laborers in Los Angeles, San

Francisco, and Redding gathered to prepare a cross-country march to Washington, D.C. The San Francisco division of 1500 men, under the leadership of "General" Charles T. Kelley, went only as far as Sacramento, where their journey came to an abrupt halt. While in Sacramento, they camped along the Southern Pacific Railroad tracks and demanded food and transportation to Reno:

> For a time the army was fed by the city of Sacramento, but after its leaders refused to board a special San Francisco-bound train, official patience began to wear thin. Eventually, amid much talk of an I.W.W. conspiracy, "General" Kelley was arrested and his army beaten back and dispersed with much brutality across the Sacramento River by volunteer deputies armed with clubs and firehoses.[9]

By the spring of 1914 the industrial and business interests of California had formed organizations for the expressed purposes of defeating unionized collective groups, preventing overt industrial disturbances and riots, and protecting their interests via the appointment of "special" policemen and the importation of strikebreakers. Some of the organizations included were the San Francisco Merchants and Manufacturers' Association, the Citizens' Alliance of Northern California, and the Stockton Merchants, Manufacturers and Employers' Association.* The concerted efforts by these commercial interests, coupled with the deepening depression and the widening class tensions, turned the earlier street disturbances into an all-out labor war throughout most of California.

At the polls, the social order of capitalism was fighting off the threatening power of socialism. In the spring of 1913 Los Angeles faced another municipal election, and again the fear of a socialist victory occupied the minds of both liberals and conservatives. In order to avoid a socialist-labor triumph by mayoral candidate Job Harriman (who had come close to

---

* In Southern California, business groups were already well organized for these purposes. For example, in Los Angeles there had prevailed for years the all-powerful "open-shop forces."

victory in the previous election), unity and cooperation were called for by the political enemies of socialism:

> Their jumpiness was clearly reflected in their readiness to indict each other for the impending disaster. In the face of the greater enemy, however, as in 1911, they temporarily resolved their differences. On March 28 the Progressives, old guard Republicans, conservative Democrats, and businessmen met in a closed meeting and heard their chairman Stoddard Jess call for united action, to follow the example of San Francisco where businessmen organized to expel McCarthyism.[10]

Despite the decline of progressive control and the upsurge of more reactionary forces everywhere else, California managed to elect a progressive governor in 1914. Nationally, however, leading candidates of the progressive party were experiencing overwhelming defeats in local and state races for office. The period of political reaction was setting in:

> "The Progressive party has come a cropper," Theodore Roosevelt remarked, after sadly surveying the national election returns in November, 1914. Ruin had come about, Roosevelt felt, because the party had gotten a reputation for radicalism from its "lunatic fringe" at the same time that the nation was rapidly swinging away from liberalism. This swing had been due, he thought, to the excesses of the radicals in the progressive movement, as well as to the current economic depression. The people had changed their interest from reform to bread-and-butter issues. They were "tired of all reformers" and especially of him. *These were revealing statements, not only about Roosevelt's reform ideology, but also about many California Progressives. It never occurred to them, as it did not to Roosevelt, that the bread-and-butter issue could be a reform issue in itself. They thought of social justice almost entirely in a political context. When the phrase was translated into economic terms it entailed "class legislation," an anathema to the average California Progressive* ... Heney's economic progressivism, as he called it, was to them Socialism, and something to be fought at whatever cost.[11] (Emphasis added)

Because of the political unrest and growing crime rates, the more powerful elements of society realized the urgent need for changes in the economic, political, social, and legal policies. Reforms in each of these spheres were primarily efforts to restore lost order and stability. The need for increased crime control was especially urgent. Consider William H. Taft's comments on the growth of criminality (April 28, 1908):

> And now, what has been the result of the lax administration of criminal law in this country? Criminal statistics are exceedingly difficult to obtain. The number of homicides one can note from the daily newspapers, the number of lynchings and the number of executions, but the number of indictments, convictions, acquittals, or mistrials it is hard to find. Since 1885, in the United States there have been 141,951 murders and homicides, and there have been 2,286 executions. In 1885 the number of murders was 1,808. In 1904 it had increased to 8,482. The number of executions in 1885 was 108. In 1904 it was 116. This startling increase in the number of murders and homicides as compared with the number of executions tells the story. As murder is on the increase, so are all offenses of the felony class, and there can be no doubt that they will continue to increase unless the criminal laws are enforced with more certainty, more uniformity, more severity than they now are.[12]

At the turn of the century, the State was forced either to stabilize the changing political economy of industrial capitalism or succumb to a new political and economic order altogether (e.g., socialism, communism). Hence, unless social control could be reinforced and strengthened, and unless crime control could be renovated and modernized, protest, violence, crime, and general chaos would continue to undermine the progress of American capitalism.

Crime Control and the Public Defender System

Arthur Train wrote in his famous book, *Courts and Criminals,* that there "exists today [1905] a widespread contempt for the criminal law which, if it has not already stimulated a general increase of criminal activity, is likely to do so in the future."[13] And Roscoe Pound, during the same period, wrote that

> increased individual self-assertion, which the last century taught us was the end to be promoted by the legal order, is still making for conscious and aggressive individual self-assertion at a time when

the general security demands that we think more of an ordered society and of common ends and less of individual freedom to do in all things as one likes.[14]

These statements typified the national sentiments toward "law and order" at the turn of the century.

During this period, a metatheory of class control developed through the writings of the founders of American sociology.[15] Social theories of anomie and disorganization, as presented by Lester Ward, Albion Small, E. A. Ross, and Robert Park of the "Chicago School" and John W. Burgess, called for a more integrated and *controlled* society.

Park and Burgess theorized that the breakdown of order and traditional relationships in society stimulated various social movements. These movements were characterized as either "normal" or "pathological." "Normal" social movements referred to activities that were directed at increased stability of the existing order. "Pathological" movements referred to activities that were directed at chaos, continued unrest, and finally, radical change. "Normal" social reforms were not threatening to the corporate order. Instead, they were designed to pacify and thus control those classes of people whose responses to the blatant inequities of the society were "pathological" (that is, disruptive to corporate capitalism). "Pathological" activities (e.g., socialistic movements, strikes), on the other hand, were threatening because they were indicative of a dangerous reluctance to recognize the legitimacy of State-defined concepts of law, order, and justice.

"Normal" criminal justice reforms were characterized by "iron-fist" and "velvet-glove" tactics.[16] "Iron-fist" or "hardline" innovations included the creation of state police, forced sterilization, in certain cases, for mentally defective persons and sex offenders, and the initiation of truancy laws. "Iron-fist" methods of crime control were obvious tools of legal intimidation.

There were, however, more subtle tactics for controlling those who, because they resented either social, economic, or political inequities, were potential threats to the growing capitalistic State. Liberal reforms were typically "velvet-glove" or "soft-line" methods of crime control. Reforms such as the PDS and JJS (Juvenile Justice System) were "democratic" reforms that helped to lend credibility to a criminal justice system that was supposedly rational and objective. In other words, the objective of most liberal reforms was to legitimize a system of law and order that was conducive to the needs of corporate capitalism.

Prior to the creation of the PDS, the ACS (Assigned Counsel System), and other adjudicative processes of criminal justice were severely criticized. Both the supporters and critics of the social and the legal orders were discussing the gross inequities suffered by the poor in the name of justice. With respect to the criminal law, especially concerning the Constitutional rights of the accused, the public was becoming aware of the injustices experienced by the less fortunate. Professor Elmer I. Miller maintained:

> The present system looks too much to victory to the powerful and too little to justice for the poor. This . . . situation must change or the rapidly declining influence of the courts with the masses of the people will soon reach a very dangerous point.[17]

To satisfy the outside criticism of the criminal defense for the poor, and to satisfy their own vested interests, legal reformers utilized the rhetoric of "due process" to incorporate State control over the adjudication of the lower classes.

More generally, the administration of criminal justice was increasingly viewed as detrimental to the "conversion" or "rehabilitation" of the "dangerous classes." According to R. H. Smith, for example, injustice to the poor created a sense of helplessness and bitterness; affirmed the belief that the law is only for the rich; led directly to open contempt for the law; encouraged fraud, dishonesty, and general lawlessness; and caused disloyalty to government and planted the seeds of anarchy. In short, Smith concludes that:

> Americanization can never make headway if such conditions are permitted to remain. For when you know, as I know, that the fa-

vorite method of extorting money from some poor wretch in jail is the representation that half of it goes to the judge, then you understand why the immigrant cannot be taught entire respect for our institutions. Experience, after all, is the final word in education.[18]

Throughout the Progressive Era, legal reformers argued that crime was flourishing and that the potential threat of criminality was increasing. The reasons for the latter were two: first, Americans were losing trust or confidence in the "American way of doing things," and consequently they were no longer committed to playing by the rules (as unemployment continued to rise and wages to decline); second, public disrespect for law was creating an atmosphere conductive to disorder, evidenced by the various groups in America who through strikes and slowdowns refused to participate in and contribute to the ongoing activity of the capitalistic nation. At the same time, disillusioned clients of the criminal justice system were pledging their allegiance to radical groups who espoused the overthrow of the government. For example, the Manly Report of the United States Commission on Industrial Relations, cited in Smith's *Justice For the Poor,* argued that one of the sources of industrial unrest was a "denial of justice in the creation, in the adjudication and in the administration of the law." Smith writes:

> The majority of our judges and lawyers view this situation with indifference. They fail to see behind this denial of justice the suffering and tragedy which it causes, the havoc it plays in individual lives and its influences in retarding our Americanization program.

> To withhold the equal protection of the laws, or to fail to carry out their intent by reason of inadequate machinery, is to undermine the entire structure and threaten it with collapse.

> It is not enough for the law to intend justice. It must be so administered that for the great body of citizens justice is actually attained. *The widespread suspicion that our law fails to secure justice has only too much basis in fact. If this suspicion is allowed to grow unchecked, it will end by poisoning the faith of the people in their own government and in law itself, the very bulwark of justice.*[19] (Emphasis added)

Legal reformers typically responded to the more obvious weaknesses of the criminal justice system. In the spirit of liberal reformism, the humanistic and benevolent changes within the administration of the criminal law played an important role in both legitimizing the corporate order and expediting the Americanization process. Thus, the PDS and other liberal reforms in the criminal justice system may be interpreted as gradual changes aimed toward class-specific crime control.

Legal Reformers, Social Order, and the Public Defender Movement

The phrase "socialism of the heart and defender of private property" could best describe most reformers, especially legal reformers, both during and after the Progressive Era. Generally speaking, reformers of the criminal justice system and those connected with the public defender movement acted implicitly with the same kind of "syndicalist" logic that explicitly guided the ruling classes (composed of a declining number of gentry and an increasing number of industrial/corporation and labor leaders). The underlying philosophy and objective social policy shared by both can be summarized as the following:

> Fully accepting the idea that private property was essential to society and individual identity, [they] took a long-range view of preserving the property by making its human aspects more equitable and its economy more efficient.[20]

Moreover, criminal justice reformers were aware of the growing importance of a rationalized and bureaucratized administration of criminal justice. These reformers were able to see the critical interrelationship between the criminal justice system (as a supporting, maintaining, and legitimating order) and the key institution of American society, corporate capitalism. Realizing that the welfare of corporate capitalism and the public interest were both inextricably bound up in the administration of the law, legal reformers set out to make the criminal justice system more efficient, economical, and humane.

All legal reformers, whether middle-class solo practitioners, legal scholars, or upper-class corporate lawyers, shared in common the marketability of ideas and the elevated status which accompanied reformers in other areas who espoused liberal ideologies, incorporated the rhetoric of progressivism, and still pledged loyalty to democratic constitutionalism. These reformers were able to become the "experts" and "specialists" for the emerging criminal justice system. Because there were many weaknesses within the administration of criminal justice, opportunities existed for new approaches and possible remedies to the increasing problems of law and order; hence, the field of criminal justice was entering the market of professionalism. And as professionalism within the system advanced, the participation of the legal profession became more involved. The legal profession was accorded status for two reasons: first, they were actively engaged in reforming the legal institutions for which the public held them responsible; and second, they were becoming members of a group of experts (e.g., crime commissions of the 20's and 30's) who possessed the philosophy, knowledge, and technical know-how to attack the growing problems of crime and delinquency.

The reformers and activists of the Progressive Era have been categorized by historians of the period from a number of perspectives: some writers have referred to reformers with respect to their political, philosophical, and ideological persuasions, while others have chosen the economic or social background of the people involved in a particular movement.[21] William A. Williams provides a combination of these approaches for distinguishing the reformers involved in the transitional period between laissez-faire and monopoly capitalism. His categories include: (1) "reactionaries"—those individuals who advocated the restoration of the laissez-faire society characteristic of the 1850's to the 1870's; (2) "radicals"—those individuals who demanded the abolishment of capitalism and advocated the establishment of a "new" kind of a social order altogether; (3) "interest-conscious corporate leaders"—individuals who favored and encouraged the corporate order with the broadest boundaries possible for the management and control of competing interests; (4) "liberal-reformers"—individuals who were moderate in approach, seeking a more balanced and equitable system with both humanitarian concern and social responsibility towards all members of society; and (5) "class-conscious corporate leaders"—individuals who argued against an "interest-oriented" order and for a regulated monopoly capitalism through a national government.[22]

With respect to the administration of criminal justice, Williams' categories and the type of people associated with each are, for the most part, discernible. However, the different reformers specifically associated with the legal and administrative development of the early modern criminal justice system can be classified more definitively as:* (1) *"Liberal reformers"*—those individuals who favored a more balanced and equitable adjudicative process for the poor when compared to the rich and called for a more humane and benevolent criminal "labeling-process"; (2) *"Social controllers"*—those individuals who sought to remove one of the sources of disintegration in American society (i.e., the "illegitimate" administration of justice in the eyes of the growing number of poor, marginal, and dissident members) and concerned themselves with the larger, but interrelated, decaying social order; and (3) *"Procedural legalists"*—those individuals who sought to alleviate the inefficiency and expense of the judicial process by attempting to reduce the

---

* It should be noted that the three groups of reformers are arbitrary. Furthermore, that it is difficult to place all individuals, groups, or organizations into a particular classification; there was much overlapping of perspectives (e.g., liberal, control, or procedural) among the various legal reformers. For example, Roscoe Pound and Felix Frankfurter could be placed in all three categories, but they were basically "social controllers" and "procedural legalists." In general, the three categories serve to emphasize the dominant perspectives of legal reformers and the individuals, groups, or organizations associated with each.

voluminous amount of dilatory maneuvers and legal technicalities, characteristic of an adversary style of justice. The idea of a PDS satisfied all three types of criminal justice reformers.

Reformers in three of Williams' categories ("interest-conscious corporate leaders," "liberal-reformers," and "class-conscious corporate leaders") accepted the emerging order of corporate capitalism and aimed their reforms at strengthening and maintaining the status quo, as did the legal reformers. Once again, the criminal justice reform movements ignored the all-important substantive areas and the property-based nature of the law.

Liberal reformers

In general, "liberal reformers" were criminal lawyers in practice for themselves, members of the middle class, and rank-and-file property owners. Examples of this group include Robert Ferrari (an independent criminal lawyer in New York City), Clara Foltz (an independent lawyer in San Francisco), Henry Forster (an independent lawyer in New York City), Mayer Goldman (an independent criminal lawyer in New York City), R. S. Gray (a criminal lawyer in San Francisco), James Reynold (a lawyer and Chairman of the Committee on the Public Defender at the 13th annual meeting of the American Institute of Criminology and Criminal Law), and R. H. Smith (a criminal lawyer in New York). Also, there were a number of newspapers and magazines throughout the country that were controlled by Progressives. Examples include: the *Los Angeles Record, Examiner, Herald,* and *Tribune* (newspapers) and *The World Outlook* of May 1914 and *The Outlook* of March 1914 (magazines). These reformers, newspapers, and magazines advocated the public defender as a fundamental Constitutional right of due process. Moreover, they all stressed the values of justice and humanity, not to mention the all-important fact that the public defender would expedite the adjudicative process.

Social controllers

"Social controllers" were members of the upper-echelons of the legal profession. Usually, they belonged to the more successful corporate law firms as partners, or at least as associate partners. Since the clients of these firms were the representatives of big business, these lawyers saw to it that their needs were satisfied in social policy. Stated differently, the various state and national crime surveys, commissions, and institutes were primarily composed of corporate attorneys; thus, not only were the interests of corporate law and the rest of the conservative legal profession served, but so were the interests and needs of the political economy of capitalism. Two noteworthy examples are:

The *Illinois Crime Survey* with Chairman Amos C. Miller and President Rush C. Butler. Miller was a partner in Miller, Gorsham, Wales, and Noxon of Chicago. This law firm specialized in corporation, commercial, and civil law. A few of its clients included the Firestone Tire and Rubber Company, the Joseph Schlitz Brewing Company, and the United States Cold Storage Company. Butler was a partner in Butler, Lamb, Forster, and Page, with law offices in Chicago and Washington, D.C. This firm specialized in corporate law.

The Cleveland Foundation: Criminal Justice in Cleveland with co-directors Alfred Bettman and Howard E. Burns. Bettman was a partner in Mouliner, Bettman and Hunt of Cincinnati (civil practice). Both Mouliner and Bettman had held public office as state attorneys. Burns was in corporate and commercial law as an associate of White, Johnson, Cannon, and Spieth of Cleveland.

The following organizations engaged in the study of the public defender issue were staffed with corporate lawyers: The Crime Commission of Michigan; the Report of the Judicial Advisory Council of Cook County; and the New York State Commission on the Administration of Justice. These committees were concerned primarily with issues of law and order and improved crime control.

Procedural legalists

"Procedural legalists" were usually scholars of the law, judges, and affiliates of the corporate legal profession. Like "social controllers," these individuals could be found on the staffs of various surveys and commissions. The following examples are of procedural-legal reformers who favored the public defender system. First, in Los Angeles there were Judges Willis, Craig, Taft, and Monroe of the Superior Court, and Judges Reeve and Summerfield of the Municipal Court. The Judicial Advisory Council of Cook County included Circuit Court Judge Fisher, and Superior Court Judges DeYoung and Sullivan. More eminent legal minds included Louis B. Brandeis, Wesley O. Howard, Arthur Train, Roscoe Pound, and Felix Frankfurter. All of these reformers shared, along with the "liberal reformers" and the "social controllers," the desire to maintain the emerging institutions of corporate capitalism, as each of these groups found themselves benefiting from such political and economic arrangements. However, these "procedural legalists" especially emphasized the importance of Constitutional reform geared towards a simpler and less cluttered procedural law. They argued that a more efficient, economical, and equitable administration of the criminal law would develop through the combined principles of applied business and cooperative law. In essence, "procedural legalists" viewed the PDS as a reform consistent with the avant-garde school of "sociological jurisprudence."

It was not until the social and legal orders were in a severe state of chaos that "social controllers" and "procedural legalists" joined the public defender movement. More than ten years had passed since Clara Foltz and other liberal reformers first introduced the PDS as a "democratic" reform. Yet, when the PDS was finally accepted as a viable reform, it was accepted not out of humanitarian concerns or guilt regarding the quality of justice for the poor. Instead, the PDS, in order to be accepted, had to be recognized as a means of improved crime control—as a reform that would support the growing interests of the capitalistic nation.

NOTES

1. Bradley Rubin, "Industrial Betterment and Scientific Management as Social Control, 1890-1920," *Berkeley Journal of Sociology,* XVII (1972-73), p. 73.
2. For general works on this period and related subject matter, see Gabriel Kolko, *The Triumph of Conservatism: A Reinterpretation of American History, 1900-1916* (Chicago: Quadrangle Books, 1967); Richard Hofstadter, *The Age of Reform: From Bryan to F.D.R.* (New York: Atheneum Press, 1965); George E. Mowry, *The California Progressives* (Chicago: Quadrangle Books, 1951); William Preston, Jr., *Aliens and Dissenters: Federal Suppression of Radicals, 1903-1933* (New York: Harper Torchbooks, 1963); James Weinstein, *The Corporate Ideal in the Liberal State, 1900-1918* (Boston: Beacon Press, 1969); William Appleman Williams, *The Contours of American History* (Chicago: Quadrangle Books, 1966); Anthony Platt, *The Child Savers: The Invention of Delinquency* (Chicago: University Press, 1966).
3. Quoted in Samuel Mencher, *Poor Law to Poverty Programs* (Pittsburgh: University Press, 1967), p. 367.
4. See generally the works of the following authors: Mencher, ibid.; John Higham, *Strangers in the Land: Patterns of American Nativism, 1860-1925* (New York: Atheneum Press, 1965); Eric F. Goldman, *Rendezvous With Destiny: A History of Modern American Reform,* revised edition (New York: Vintage Books, 1955).
5. Preston, *Aliens and Dissenters,* p. 44.
6. Daniel Bell, "The Background and Development of Marxian Socialism in the U.S.," *Socialism and American Life* (Princeton: Princeton University Press, 1952), I, pp. 213-405.
7. Mowry, *California Progressives,* p. 196.
8. Ibid., p. 197.
9. Ibid., p. 198.
10. Ibid., pp. 201-02.
11. Ibid., p. 217.
12. Quoted in *The Journal of Criminal Law and Criminology,* VI (1915-1916), p. 378.
13. Arthur Train, *Courts and Criminals* (New York: Scribner's, 1924), p. 214.
14. Roscoe Pound, *Criminal Justice in America* (New York: Henry Holt and Co., 1930), p. 169.
15. See generally the works of Lester Ward, *Dynamic Sociology* (New York: D. Appleton and Co., 1883), 2 vols., and *Applied Sociology* (Boston: Ginn and Co., 1906); Albion Small, *General Sociology* (Chicago: University of Chicago Press, 1905); E. A. Ross, *Foundations of Sociology* (New York: The Macmillan Co., 1905). And for a critical review of the "founding fathers" of American sociology, see Herman and Julia Schwendinger, *Sociologists of the Chair* (New York: Basic Books, 1974).

16. *The Iron Fist and Velvet Glove,* ed. by The Center for Research on Criminal Justice (Berkeley: CRCJ, 1975).

17. Quoted in R. S. Gray, "The Advisability of a Public Defender," *The American Academy of Political and Social Science, Reform in the Administration of Justice,* p. 180.

18. R. H. Smith, "Denial of Justice," *Journal of American Judicature Society,* III, December 1919, p. 180.

19. R. H. Smith, *Justice and the Poor* (New York: The Carnegie Foundation for the Advancement of Teaching, 1919), Bulletin No. 13, pp. 5, 9, and xi-xii.

20. Williams, *Contours of American History,* p. 392.

21. For examples see Joseph R. Gusfield, *Symbolic Crusade: Status Politics and the American Temperance Movement* (Urbana: University of Illinois Press, 1963); Hofstader, *Act of Reform,* and Platt, *The Child Savers.*

22. Williams, *Contours of American History,* pp. 372–376.

5 THE EQUAL JUSTICE IDEAL: Liberation

Procedural safeguards were created to protect the democratic character of our criminal legal system. They were designed to protect the accused individual who alone faces the collective resources of the State. The concept of due process required procedural guarantees that would protect the accused from arbitrary and whimsical misapplications of the law.

Historically, the essence of criminal justice was captured in the Massachusetts Bill of Rights of 1780: "It is essential to the preservation of the rights of every individual, his life, liberty, property, and character, that there be an impartial interpretation of the laws and the administration of justice." A few years later, the Bill of Rights expounded and elaborated upon the notions of individual justice and rights.

One of the procedural safeguards recognized in the Bill of Rights was the right to counsel. The Sixth Amendment (1791) reads in part:

> In all criminal prosecutions, the accused shall enjoy the right to a speedy and public trial . . . and to have the Assistance of Counsel for his defense.

The right to counsel was regarded as an important right because, in many cases, the accused was unable to match the legal prowess of the State. Specifically, it was necessary to guarantee the accused right to counsel because, in most cases, the accused was:

(1) Unable to judge if the indictment [was] valid;

(2) Incapable of analyzing and selecting an appropriate defense strategy to the charge;

(3) Incapable of selecting the witnesses for cross-examination, catching improper introduction of evidence by the prosecutor, objecting to questions put to witnesses and improper comment to the jury.[1]

Defense counsel was also regarded as necessary to an equitable administration of justice under the notion that the criminal courtroom exists as the neutral/democratic battleground for the State's quest for truth and the accused's need for justice. For the battle to be fair and democratic, it was essential that the accused be defended by someone who knew and understood the law.

In the past century, however, this concept of criminal proceedings as an adversarial situation has withered away; in its place has emerged the bureaucratic model of criminal justice. Abraham Blumberg describes bureaucratic justice as it relates to idealistic notions of due process:

While the constitutional ideology of due process and rule of law is proclaimed as the mode of justice we exalt and revere, it is a perfunctory, administrative-bureaucratic version of due process that has been implemented in our criminal courts. "Bureaucratic due process" serves as bland obeisance to constitutional principles. It is characterized by the superficial ceremonies and formal niceties of traditional due process, but not its substance. It consists of strategies and evasions calculated to induce pleas of guilty, and it has become the truly viable system of criminal justice in America.[2]

Similarly, Jerome Skolnick has written:

While the adversary system contemplates an aggressive defense, the "cooperative" system alters the nature of the services that the defense attorney is capable of performing for his client.

[And furthermore, if] the adversary system is defined with only the trial in mind, we are blinding ourselves to the realities of a system of decision that is predominantly pretrial in character. These pretrial proceedings are played out against a background of court congestion, eliciting the prominence of administrative concerns as compared to institutionally guaranteed participation from the point of view of those with "interests" in the proceeding, at least four parties seem to be involved in the system—the complainant, the prosecutor, the defendant, the defense attorney. From this perspective, the ideas of representation and of a "side" become problematic, since the long-term self-interest of the professionals in the system seems to influence the character of their participation in any given proceeding. Under such circumstances, adjudication does not define the adversary system, but is instead the outcome of a failure of negotiation between attorney and client as between defense and prosecution.[3]

According to the two quotations cited above, idealized principles of justice bear little reality to the present character of our criminal justice system. Also, as Blumberg explains further, that which is now considered rational in the administration of justice need not be that which is fundamentally fair or just:

The concern with better and more extensive rules has served as a facade of moral philosophy to divert our gaze from the more significant development of the emergence of "bureaucratic due process," a non-adversary system of justice by negotiation. It consists of secret bargaining sessions, employing subtle, bureaucratically ordained modes of coercion and influence to dispose of onerously large case loads in an efficacious and "rational" manner.[4]

Whether the administration of law is based on an adversarial or bureaucratic scheme, it is commonly assumed that the right of the accused to counsel is an inalienable right. Yet, in an adversarial situation, defense counsel was initially regarded as supplying the necessary balance between the State and the accused individual; from the standpoint of "bureaucratic due process," however, defense counsel exists, to use Blumberg's phrase, as a necessary "facade of moral philosophy."

The essence of criminal justice today is to be found, as Blumberg and Skolnick maintain, in a co-opted version of "bureaucratic due process." It is also generally conceded that since organizational variables and not idealized principles define the quality of justice in America today, the administration of the law is anything but blind. Yet, despite this realization, the same false logic that underpinned the efforts of the liberal reformers during the Progressive Era still misguides the efforts of criminal justice reformers today. The assumption still exists that there is a consensus or harmony of interests among social classes in a capitalist society: that which is beneficial to the economy, the criminal justice system and the corporate-legal sector, is naturally beneficial to both the practitioners and clients of criminal justice.

Gideon v. *Wainwright*

Even though the right to counsel was recognized early in this country's history as a fundamental right, only in the past forty-six years have the courts acted to extend the meaning of this right. In *Powell* v. *Alabama*[5] (1932), the states were required to supply counsel in all capital cases and in cases in which the defendant was incapable of defending himself because of "ignorance, feeblemindedness, illiteracy, or the like." In *Johnson* v. *Zerbs*[†6] (1934), the right to an assigned counsel was extended to include all accused indigents in Federal courts. But the decision in *Betts* v. *Brady*[7] twelve years later took a step backward. The *Betts* rule maintained that representation by counsel was not a requirement essential to a fair trial. It was not until *Gideon* v. *Wainwright*[8] in 1963 that the Warren Court reversed the *Betts* decision in felony trials.

In effect, *Gideon* required that the courts furnish counsel in all felony cases of indigent defendants. Subsequently, *Escobedo*[9] (1964) and *Miranda*[10] (1966) expanded the right to counsel even further. As a result of these two decisions, an accused individual is entitled to the right to either retained or appointed counsel preceding any interrogation by police. Finally, the Supreme Court declared in *Argersinger* v. *Hamlin*[11] (1972) that the right extends to persons who are charged with any crime for which prison is a potential penalty.

By reason of *Gideon* v. *Wainwright,* most people would agree that the right to counsel is meaningless as long as it is contingent upon the accused's ability to hire an attorney. Most people would assert that an individual is unjustly treated, regardless of his guilt or innocence, if he is not provided with some kind of legal representation at his trial.

In the past twenty years, the PDS has salved the public conscience in regard to justice for the poor; the indigent, assured of legal representation, stands on equal footing with the State. Because balance is provided between the State and the accused, treatment of the accused is regarded as fair and just. Because the PDS has served to justify our current system of justice, it is now an established legal institution.

Specifically, the PDS as an institution within the criminal justice system has expanded for the following reasons: the recent state supreme court and U.S. Supreme Court decisions concerning the fundamental right to counsel; the continuing growth of state bureaucracies, along with the increasing size of the civil service labor force; the sustained efforts to centralize and rationalize the system of criminal justice; and the rising number of criminal cases and the disproportionate number of poor people unable to afford private counsel.[12]

Although the PDS has been accepted as a viable part of our criminal justice system, it still remains a topic for controversy. Preconceived notions of the public defender's responsibilities, along with criticisms of the type of defense strategies employed by the office, provide the ground for arguments in favor of and opposed to the PDS. For example, consider Platt and Pollock's description of the public's concept of who and what the public defender is:

> Public Defenders, like other sectors of the law enforcement labor force, have been victimized by . . . stereotyping. They are either uncritically celebrated by government and professional authorities as indispensible public servants or they are depicted by critics and muckrakers as lackeys of prosecutors or, at best, dangerous do-gooders.[13]

Briefly, the arguments in favor of the public defender are as follows: he fulfills the right of counsel for all indigent defendants in an efficient and economical manner; he settles the majority of cases through pleas of guilty (the same as most criminal attorneys); he grows intimate and expert in dealings with the prosecutor so that the two can arrive at a negotiated bargain which is beneficial to both; and he utilizes a "law office approach," employing attorneys who come to specialize in various aspects of procedural and criminal law, and who are equipped with a full range of resources for developing a competent defense strategy. Conversely, the negative arguments are that the public defender is subject to political and/or judicial corruption; he is employed by the State, and therefore, reflects a conflict of interests; and he is limited to working within the boundaries of a closed community whose organizational pressures necessitate compromise.

The following excerpts indicate the central issues associated with criminal defense work.* After comparing public and private attorneys, Gerald Smith concludes that ". . . public defenders are generally just as effective as private attorneys in settling criminal matters."[14] In contrast, the authors of "Civil Justice and the Poor" argue that:

> Neither the assigned counsel nor public defender system as now constituted is capable of providing adequate service to the indigent accused. A large proportion of poor defendants (particularly in misdemeanor cases) are not represented at all. Moreover, when counsel is provided he frequently has neither the resources, the skill nor the incentive to defend his client effectively; and he usually enters the case too late to make any real difference in the outcome.[15]

And David Sudnow, in a criticism based on his study of the PDS, asserts that the public defender "will not cause any serious trouble for the routine notion of the court conviction process." He claims that:

> Laws will not be challenged, cases will not be tried to test the constitutionality of procedures and statutes, judges will not be personally degraded, police will be free from scrutiny to decide the legitimacy of their operations, and the community will not be con-

---

* Other liberal issues associated with the administration of criminal justice are the notion of a "due process" model v. a "crime control" model of law enforcement; the correctional dichotomy of punishment and treatment; and the utility/rationality of "assembly-line" justice v. the democratic/philosophic ideal of justice.

demned for its segregative practices against Negroes. The P.D.'s defense is completely proper, in accord with correct legal procedure, and specifically amoral in its import, manner of delivery, and perceived implications for the propriety of the prosecution enterprise.

In "return" for all this, the district attorney treats the defendant's guilt in a matter-of-fact fashion, doesn't get hostile in the course of the proceedings, doesn't insist that the jury or judge "throw the book" but rather "puts on a trial" (in their way of referring to their daily tasks) in order to, with a minimum of strain, properly place the defendant behind bars. Both prosecutor and public defender thus protect the moral character of the other's charges from exposure.[16]

Skolnick replies to Sudnow that even though the adversary system of criminal justice is actually a cooperative system, the quality of criminal defense law is not altered by these social relationships:

Administrative requirements characterizing the American administration of criminal justice make for a reciprocal relationship between prosecutor and defense attorney that strains toward cooperation; that this relationship is based upon interests wider than those of the parties they represent, the State and the accused; that the public defender, as an institution, does not significantly differ from other "cooperative" defense attorneys; and that the dilemma of the adversary system arises from the fact that such tendencies toward "cooperation"—under existing conditions—do not demonstrably impede the quality of representation.[17]

Edward Bennett Williams disagrees with Skolnick:

The public defender and prosecutor are trying cases against each other every day. They begin to look at their work like two wrestlers who wrestle with each other in a different city every night and in time get to be good friends. The biggest concern of the wrestlers is to be sure they do not hurt each other too much. They don't want to get hurt. They just want to make a living. Apply that to the public defender and the prosecutor situation and it is not a good thing in a system of justice that is based upon the adversary system.[18]

And finally, the succinct statements of Blumberg:

The lawyer, whether a public defender or a privately retained defense counsel, is subject to pressures peculiar to his role and organizational obligations. But ultimately he is also concerned with

strategies leading to a plea. Again, impersonal elements prevail—
the economics of time, labor, expense, and the commitment of the
defense counsel to the rationalistic values of the court organization; the accused who expects a personal, affective relationship is
likely to be disappointed. . . . Indeed, adversary features are for the
most part muted and exist in their attenuated form largely for ex-
ternal consumption. The principals—lawyer and assistant district
attorney—rely upon each other's cooperation for their continued
professional existence, and so the bargaining between them usually
is "reasonable" rather than fierce.[19]

Conventional analyses of both the American system of
criminal justice and the public defender system suffer from a
lack of historical perspective. Social scientists of the law
have consistently failed to acknowledge that the PDS, the
same as other institutions in the criminal justice enterprise,
has been more than peripherally affected by economic, social, and political forces. The history of the public defender
movement and the early origins of the public defender office
are typically ignored. For instance:

Whatever the reasons for its development, we now find in many
urban places a public defender occupying a place alongside judge
and prosecutor as a regular court employee.[20]

In order to understand the criminal defense of an indigent
accused of committing a crime, the literature alleges that
the public defender is a relatively new phenomenon, tracing
the office's beginnings to recent court decisions. For example, Blumberg maintains that:

Unlike most of the rest of the nation prior to the *Gideon* v.
Wainwright decision requiring counsel in all felony cases, no person who appears in Metropolitan Court is ever without the assistance of a lawyer at every stage of his case.[21]

And Sudnow notes:

As the accused is, by law, entitled to the aid of counsel, and as his
pocketbook is often empty, numerous cities have felt obliged to establish a public defender system.[22]

Generally, the foregoing analyses accept as static the
composition of the American legal profession, the judicial

organization of the administration of criminal law, and the institution of the public defender. In other words, the *stratification* of the legal profession, the *bureaucratization* of the criminal justice system, and the *institutionalization* of the public defender are treated independent of each other's historical development. Hence, explanations of the development of these institutions in relationship to each other, let alone in relationship to theories of change[23] or the State[24] have typically been ignored or dismissed.

Typically, the differences between private and public defense lawyers are largely viewed as insignificant. It is commonly assumed that in the average criminal case, the public defender is equal in quality and competence to the average private attorney practicing criminal law. The traditional approach for evaluating the distribution of justice has been: does the indigent defendant receive essentially the same kind of legal defense that the nonindigent receives? This approach, however, ignores the following facts: first, that the creation and initiation of the PDS was the result of a *legislative,* and not a *judicial,* act in 1913; second, that the arguments ultimately bringing about the implementation of the public defender revolved around the issues of "law and order," not humanitarian motives; third, that the relative infrequency of nonindigents coming in contact with the criminal side of the law makes the comparative distinction between justice for the poor and justice for the rich a useless base for evaluation; and fourth, that the most skilled members of the legal profession were exempted from the traditional obligation of representing uncounseled defendants on behalf of the court.

The effect of having the State act as both the public agency for the offense (prosecutor) and the defense (public defender) has also been overlooked. In reference to both the motives and interests involved in criminal adjudication, attorney Bob Wolf states:

I know everyone (prosecutors, judges, public defenders) means well and I know there is no attempt being made to keep private prac-

titioners in the dark. It's just that the public defender is always included where we're not, because the public defender handles the
bulk of the criminal cases. But we in private practice are still here,
and I think we need to be considered, too, when the judges hold
their meetings and make policy changes.[25]

The private criminal lawyer is kept "in the dark" because
of this monopolistic partnership—that is, the State, acting as
both the offense and defense, works to the disadvantage of
criminal lawyers. For example, a Las Vegas attorney has
proposed that a criminal defense lawyers association be
formed so private practitioners can enjoy the same privileges
as public defenders and prosecutors when it comes to being
informed on courthouse policy.[26]

In short, the paradoxical interests of this unique partnership between the prosecutor and the public defender have
usurped the adversarial system of the nineteenth century,
substituting the present system of "bargain" justice for
"everybody." The public defender, unlike the accused indigent, is capable of "bargaining" because he, like the prosecutor, knows the law and how to manipulate it. Unfortunately, it is rarely acknowledged that the bargain struck by
the public defender more often than not reflects the interests of the State and not those of the accused. At the same
time, it goes unsaid that for the accused who can afford private counsel, "bargain" justice, more often than not, can
work nicely to his advantage.

The PDS and Repressive Justice

Through the paternalism of local governments or corporate foundations, corporate justice is provided for the poor,
Third World, and working-class members of America.
Hence, in criminal as well as non-criminal law, legal strategies for the problems and needs of the poor are designed
within the framework of corporate capitalism, by outsiders
with differing, if not antagonistic, concerns. Accordingly, we
witness the PDS and other liberal reforms hindering the development of policies beneficial to the poor while, at the

same time, helping to sustain a legal order which is blind to the political realities of justice by class or race:

> Public defender systems fail, not because they are impersonal bureaucracies and not because they are severely underfinanced, but primarily because their programs are administrative: their purpose is to process the underclass through the courts on a mass basis. The assigned counsel system masks its class bias behind legal professionalism, but public defender systems make no pretense: its lawyers are full-time advocates for the poor. Yet the ties between the public defenders and the court hierarchy are necessarily intimate, so that class conflict is reduced to an administrative process: the cooperative effort reveals the class and racial basis of legal aid paternalism.[27]

Within the criminal justice system, the public or private defense lawyers for the poor are typically members of the legal profession who: (1) rank lowest in education, status, power, and skill; (2) do not fulfill the constitutional role of adversary, but instead serve as servants of the State, protecting the class interests of bourgeois legal institutions; (3) have already assumed the guilt of indigent clients; and (4) contribute to the *appearance* of due process of law while serving the *real* needs of the State.

By contrast, the rich and influential members of American society benefit from the policies of today's criminal justice system. Thus, the position is taken by the legal profession that while corporate organizations and people with property need the law, it is of limited use to the indigent:

> While the profession offers legal services to the upper classes for every conceivable thing—preventive research, preparing contracts [trusts, estates, managing and investing money, developing tax loopholes, etc.]—it generally assumes that the problems of the poor are basically nonlegal and essentially . . . social, or psychological in character.[28]

The legal profession of today still thinks, as it did at the turn of the century, of social justice almost entirely within a political context. The legal and economic arrangements that have served to perpetuate the exploitative aspects of the political economy, which are responsible for all forms of aggregate criminality, have been ignored by criminal justice reformers. In the words of Representative John Conyers, Jr., D-Michigan, Chairman of the House Subcommittee on Crime:

> America's entire crime-fighting establishment is in near ruin, as are the premises about the nature of crime which underpin it. For years no one has had an original analysis of the problem nor has anyone proposed an innovative solution.

> And so, despite grand schemes and even grander federal budgets to aid local police, such as those recommended by the last three Chief Executives, crime has gone ever upward.

> Even though official statistics underreport crime (and ignore altogether crimes not committed in the streets), they do indicate the awesome trends. From 1965 to 1975, the murder rate . . . increased 165 per cent; aggravated assault . . . rose 195 per cent. During this same period, combined state and federal spending to fight crime shot up from $4.2 billion per year to more than $17.2 billion in 1975.

> Why must this be in the most affluent society the world has known?

> If you take a long [historical] look (and, for the moment, set aside morality), you quickly find one answer: stealing has always been a means of redistributing the wealth. I'll grant you it has been a risky and inefficient technique, but who can deny that it has paid off for some practitioners.

> The main difference between crime of the past and the present is that more of it is going on now. Given this epidemic, our means of combating crime makes little sense. Instead of taking the initiative and redistributing the wealth in a fairer fashion, we arrest those [index offenders] who make the effort on their own and put them in prison—even though our experience of the past decade indicates that stricter law enforcement has little effect on the crime rate. (Capital punishment, mandatory and minimum sentencing satisfy the appetite of some for revenge, but do little else.)

> I submit that the question of crime is not, How do we reduce the crime rate in our cities? It is rather, How shall we reorder our cities so that crime is not a built-in part of the system?

> After all, crime is not primarily caused by criminals, outlandish though that may sound. Crime in the aggregate is more fundamentally the product of desperation brought on by joblessness, poverty

and community disintegration. Criminal acts multiply when a neighborhood or a city—even a nation—has so degenerated in its ability to provide for the well-being of people that individuals feel that stealing, mugging or selling dope is an acceptable means of survival. In short, crime is the economic and political consequence of a system rooted in indifference toward, and exploitation of, marginal and disadvantaged people.

When a community begins to be starved of the jobs, public institutions and social services it needs to survive (once a neighborhood is defined as a high crime area, services disappear at an alarming rate), and when its members are so desperate they must fend for themselves—that's when a community loses the chance to flex enough political muscle to fight for the larger social goals necessary to effect a turnabout.

Meanwhile, law-abiding citizens become victims of criminals as well as crime-fighters:

—Victims of the numbers racketeers, loan sharks and dope pushers who prey on despair and dreams of people without hope.

—Victims also of the massive and heavily armed police forces which every year suck up billions of dollars from the public purse, grow more and more to resemble occupying forces, and are increasingly used to destroy any indigenous political movements by which citizens might really attack the problems of crime in their neighborhoods.[29]

Generally speaking, as Conyers indicates, the law provides only remedial services for the poor and working-class. In other words, these classes of people receive legal guidance, whether for criminal or civil matters, only after arrests, or after property has been repossessed, or after welfare agencies have neglected to abide by various codes and regulations. In short, the upper classes have lawyers to look after their property needs whereas the lower classes, as a result of their lack of property, also lack the attorneys to see to their particular economic, political, and social needs.

Finally, the PDS as it now exists demands attorneys who are apolitical and status-quo oriented; all others are likely to find themselves frustrated and embittered.[30] Only those who act as agents of the State, not the community they serve, are able to survive. Their clients, recognizing the true allegiance of the PD attorneys, often become cynical and distrustful regarding the aid provided. Thus, we have mutual suspicion and contempt between lawyer and client. Such a situation does not exist, nor could it ever be tolerated, between corporate lawyers and their clients.

The Bankruptcy of Liberalism and Crime Control

During the past ten years—in response to the decline in worldwide political and economic dominance of the United States—we have been witnessing the bankruptcy of liberal crime control strategies. Perhaps nothing brings home this realization as much as the execution of Gary Gilmore in 1977 by a Utah firing squad, signifying the re-establishment of the death penalty. Within forty-eight hours after the State carried out this execution, Senate Bill 45 was introduced in the Nevada Senate. The bill "would allow a person sentenced to life in prison without the possibility of parole to ask to be put to death.[31] Bill Hernstadt, a freshman Democrat, president/owner of a local television station in Las Vegas, and one of the principal sponsors of the bill, argued that the main purpose was to save money for Nevada taxpayers:

> This relieves Nevada taxpayers from having to support a person for the rest of his life. It could cost the taxpayers an average of $250,000 to keep a person in jail for 20 years.[32]

Unfortunately, Mr. Hernstadt is not alone. Not only does he have the support of other politicians and lay persons, but also that of both practitioners and theoreticians of crime and crime control.

Liberal criminologists are moving further to the right. In particular, if we look at various theoretical and ideological preferences, we notice the rebirth of a movement toward anti-intellectualism and conservatism even among liberal scholars. With LEAA providing more funds for *crime-control* related research rather than for *change-oriented* research, there seems to be little, if any, concern for understanding the causes, needs, and structures of American crime.

Old questions and concepts of classical utilitarianism, which have laid dormant for years, are now being rejuvenated. Not too long ago the "rehabilitative ideal" was adamantly supported by liberal criminologists. At that time, the conservative criminologists who advocated capital punishment and stiffer sentencing practices, and who believed in the value of imprisonment as a deterrent, were ridiculed by their liberal counterparts. Today, their seemingly different positions can be viewed as blending into a technocratic perspective which favors the deterrent theory. Also, consider James Q. Wilson's contention that theories of crime provide little, if any, guidance for pragmatic policy makers:

> Explaining human behavior is a worthwhile endeavor; indeed, for intellectuals it is among the most worthwhile. Those who search for such explanations *need not justify their activity by its social utility or its policy implications.* . . . To a degree, of course, criminological knowledge may assist criminologist's action: careful study and conscientious learning can help one avoid obvious error, attack popular myths, and devise inventive proposals. But it is also likely that the most profound understanding may impede or even distort, rather than facilitate, choice, because much of this knowledge is of what is immutable and necessary, not of what is variable or contingent.[33] (Emphasis added)

Seymour Halleck, a "part-time" criminologist by his own admission, in writing the introduction to *The Aldine Crime and Justice Annual* (1974) notes that "perspectives in criminology have drastically changed in the last few years."[34] Yet, Halleck confidently asserts that the field of criminal justice will remain much as it is although "the question ['what works?'] is now predominant, whether one is concerned with healing or controlling."[35]

There is, however, an increasing number of "radical," or more accurately *critical* criminologists who are now asking the fundamental questions of criminology: "Why do we have the kind of crime which presently exists?" "What are the relationships between this crime and the legal order, the

State, and the political economy?" and finally, "What is the quality of justice which exists, and what are the consequences of our present strategies of crime control?"

Toward Social Justice

Richard Quinney and John Wildeman in their last section of *The Problem of Crime,* conclude that a true "struggle for social justice" is only *possible* when one realizes that:

Any social problem, crime included, is understandable only if it is seen within the framework of the social, economic, and political structure of the society. We are convinced that the problem of crime in the United States is really the problem of capitalist society. Consequently, the crime problem in the United States cannot be solved within the context of the political economy of capitalism.

Earlier we projected one possible future for American society: oppressive and totalitarian, a frozen and permanent alienation. But we do not close on this note; for these things, as all things social, are dialectical in nature. An emergence of freedom from bondage, of optimism from pessimism, is always on the edge of the possible.

The alternative tomorrow that we have also been suggesting, then, is indeed possible. This is a world freed from the dehumanizing conditions and contradictions of capitalism, freed from the brutality of class oppression, hierarchy, and domination. Only then can we begin to adequately consider solutions to the problems of crime.

Such a world comes to pass only through socialist, revolutionary struggle. That the struggle has already begun is indicated by a widespread discontent among the American people; by emergent liberation movements in all oppressed groups; by the gradual withdrawal of legitimacy from the institutions of society; by the growing critical imagination; and by everyday struggles in the community and in places of the world. All of these are part of the struggle for a new world, one in which class divisions are no longer present and one in which a capitalist system will be replaced by a *more efficient and humane organization.*

We are engaged in a common struggle, a struggle of truly historical significance, against the oppressions and contradictions of the capitalist state and economy. What the new socialist society to be born from that struggle will look like can be known only in the struggle for social justice. But it will be a society dedicated to our common existence. It will be a world relieved of the burden of crime as we know it today in the United States.[36] (Emphasis added)

This work has implied that the *uncritical* models of crime and crime control (e.g., conventional criminology) view the individual, law, and society from a microscopic, technocratic, and ahistorical perspective. In short, the theory and the practice of the conventional analysis of crime control and the administration of criminal justice narrowly reduce the problems of criminality to the maintenance of the existing order through corporate justice. The primary concern of conventional criminologists has been to answer the following questions: How does society improve the formally institutionalized methods and techniques of crime control? How does society create a more efficient and effective system of "democratic" criminal justice? *In essence, what are the most appropriate strategies for reinforcing present social relations in American society?*

Answers to such questions are typically formulated within the framework of a legality which, in turn, can be characterized by specific extra-legal assumptions. First, the ideology of capitalist legality assumes that particular social, political, and economical problems (e.g., the production and allocation of services, the distribution of wealth and power, and the maintenance of privilege and repression) are separate and distinct; that is, they are held to be unrelated to some central totality, such as the political economy of a sociohistorical period. Second, it is assumed that existing crises (e.g., unemployment, inflation, social security, and health care) are the products of past mistakes, improper judgments, and random cases of individualized anomalies. Lastly, it is assumed that the government is a detached and disinterested body responding to those needs that provide for the welfare of all citizens and, therefore, that it should be actively solicited and engaged in mitigating the antagonisms of advanced capitalism (e.g., wealth/poverty, profits/people, equality/discrimination, technology/environmental destruction).

By contrast, criminologists supporting the New Criminology are now developing a macroscopic framework that has already started to integrate the needs and problems of society and its institutions. The New Criminology examines the *quality* of the human condition and justice in America, rather than merely increasing the number of mechanisms by which social injustice is controlled; it questions the equity of our political and economic institutions, instead of accepting and perpetuating them unquestioningly. Born amidst the political struggles of the sixties and propelled by the crises of post-industrial capitalism, the New Criminology is grounded in the methodologies of historical materialism, emphasizing the study of the distribution of power in a dialectically changing social order—the study of systems of exploitation and oppression operating through the administration of present-day criminal justice.

Given this conceptual orientation, the New Criminology demystifies conventional interpretations of the State and of "law and order" by placing both of them in the context of the political economy of capitalism. Equally important, the New Criminology exposes the different legal myths which legitimize the State's monopoly over the use of force, penal sanctions, and territoriality.[37] In explaining the contradictions between individual or distributive justice and social or equitable justice—between the ideal, formal and rational law and the real, informal and substantive law—the New Criminology has begun to make the necessary connections between what C. Wright Mills terms *personal troubles and public issues*.[38] In the process, emphasis on "crime" is shifted away from the individual and private concern toward the institutional and public concern. The New Criminology sees the possibilities of gradually changing criminal codes, not through piece-meal juridical quibbles, but through political struggle. At the same time, it also sees the possibilities of creating and/or expanding other laws which could help

to shield people from racial and sexual discrimination, pollution, misuse of public resources, manufacture and sale of defective products, deceptive advertising and packaging, commercial housing and insurance fraud, violations of safety codes, stock manipulations, tax violations [and other white-collar, corporate, and governmental crimes.][39]

When discussing the possibilities of non-repressive justice and alternative social orders, the New Criminology argues that there is a need to escape the narrow confines of the legalistic definition of crime—a definition that confines conventional criminologists to the study and ultimate control of only legally defined criminals who, according to the New Criminologists, may not be the real criminals at all. In other words, when trying to explain anti-social or injurious behavior in society, the legalistic definition of crime may actually deflect our attention from the more serious criminality of a capitalist society. Unlike the police who enforce the laws, the legal professionals who carry out the law, and the conventional criminologists who support and rationalize the existing legal order, critical criminologists are not bound by the State's definition of crime. As criminologists, they feel that their obligation is not only to explain why specific types of behavior are labeled criminal while other types more injurious to the well-being of society are not, but also to note and account for disparities and differences between the "official" world of criminal justice and the "real" world of justice administration as found in their research. After examining these contradictions, the New Criminologists have reformulated problems of crime and crime control. And these reformulations have, in turn, begun to move us closer to the necessary ideological and structural changes required for the achievement of social justice.

The critical analysis argues that crime must be defined in such a way that it reflects the reality of a legal system based on power and privilege.[40] Or stated differently, critical criminologists argue that to accept the legal definition of crime is to accept the *fiction* of "neutral" law rather than the *fact* of law as an expression of class and group interests. Thus, Julia and Herman Schwendinger in 1970 offered a humanistic definition of crime as one alternative. They defined crime as the *violation of politically defined human rights* (e.g., the right to decent food and shelter, human dignity and sense of community, self-determination).[41]

The human rights definition of crime allows us to study as primary to the investigation of "crime" the various relationships and practices of a legal order and larger society where the right to compete for unequal shares of wealth and power contributes to both social injury and human misery. The New Criminology not only studies the victims of exploitation, but also focuses attention on criminogenic conditions so that strategies can be devised for resisting further victimization of marginal members of society.

Ignoring the larger relationships between the individual and the socio-economic order that structures his existence (as conventional criminologists have done), or studying the system of institutional crimes without acknowledging the offenders, victims, and regulators, stems from cynicism or idealism, neither of which can bring about necessary social change.[42] A classic example of this is the issue of civil rights, the Supreme Court, and Black liberation. The study of discrimination in America divorced from both the historical and the underlying political and economic realities of the social participants (e.g., the oppressor, the oppressed, and the enforcer) could lead to the idealistic conclusion that the law and the U.S. Constitution are the vehicles for Black emancipation. Conversely, given the limited social progress that Blacks have made after one-hundred years of litigation, one could cynically conclude that racism is an inevitable part of the human condition. Both of these conclusions are incorrect. First, the Constitution might be a vehicle for legal equality, but it is certainly not a mechanism for political and economic equality—the prerequisites for social justice and human emancipation. Second, racism is not an inevitable part of the human condition, but rather the socio-historical expression of the political and economic arrangements of capitalism.

Currently, critical criminologists are breaking free from traditional criminology by organizing educational conferences, establishing new curricula and internship programs, supporting defendants in political trials, and helping to sustain and develop indigenous programs of community control that act to: (1) integrate the "personal" troubles of fragmented communities and atomized individuals with the "public" issues of the socio-historical period; (2) bridge the schism between the *real* and the *academic* worlds; and (3) expose the relationships between, for example, racism and crime, sexism and crime, and corporate liberalism and the emergence of a modern system of crime control.

As far as specific issues are concerned, the New Criminology examines and evaluates the consequences of suggested reforms and social policies in criminal justice. Again, the perspective chosen is that of the people, not that of the State, the political economy, and various hegemonic groups in society. In other words, the New Criminology argues that *more* is not necessarily *better* crime control. In fact, the historical experience of American penology tells us otherwise:

> Although the expansion of probationary staffs, TASC programs, halfway houses, bail policies, and earlier parole releases may be considered as means of ameliorating the problems of expensive, overcrowded, and decaying institutions, these liberal reforms are doing little, if any, good for convicted offenders, either in terms of integrating them into society or in terms of alleviating some of the underlying conditions responsible for their criminality.[43]

The New Criminology is not interested in increasing and improving techniques of formal crime control as the informal means of social control continue to atrophy in our communities. It is, instead, interested in understanding the nature and various forms of criminality as well as explaining the origins, developments, and operations of both informal and formal mechanisms of social control. In striving to do this, critical criminologists work toward the creation of a society where the need for formal means of social control has been reduced by the institutionalization of laws for the protection of human and public interests rather than private and class interests.

NOTES

1. Gerald Wayne Smith, "A Comparative Examination of the Public Defender and Private Attorneys in a Major California County," (Ph.D. dissertation, University of California, 1969), pp. 34–35.
2. Abraham Blumberg, *Criminal Justice* (Chicago: Quadrangle, 1967), p. 4.
3. Jerome H. Skolnick, "Social Control and the Adversary System," *The Journal of Conflict Resolution,* XI, March 1967, pp. 52–70.
4. Blumberg, *Criminal Justice,* p. 21.
5. *Powell v. Alabama,* 287 U.S. 45, 77 L.Ed. 1461, 53 S. Ct. 1019, 1932.
6. *Johnson v. Zerbst,* 304 U.S. 458, 82 L.Ed. 1461, 58 S. Ct. 1019, 1938.
7. *Betts v. Brady,* 316 U.S. 455, 86 L.Ed. 1595, 62 S. Ct. 1252, 1942.
8. *Gideon v. Wainwright,* 372 U.S. 335, 9 L.Ed. 2d 799, 83 S. Ct. 792, 1963.
9. *Escobedo v. Illinois,* 378 U.S. 478, 12 L.Ed. 2d 977, 84 S. Ct. 1958, 1964.
10. *Miranda v. Arizona,* 384 U.S. 436, 16 L.Ed. 2d 694, 84 S. Ct. 1602, 1966.
11. *Argersinger v. Hamlin,* 92 S. Ct. 2006 (1972).
12. Anthony Platt and Randy Pollock, "Channeling Lawyers: The Careers of Public Defenders," *Issues in Criminology,* IX, Spring 1974, p. 32.
13. Ibid.
14. Smith, "A Comparative Examination of the Public Defender," p. 204.
15. Jerome E. Carlin, Jon Howard, and Sheldon Messinger, "Civil Justice and the Poor: Issues for Sociological Research," *Law and Society Review,* I, November 1966, p. 56.
16. David Sudnow, "Normal Crimes: Sociological Features of the Penal Code in a Public Defender's Office," in *Crime and Justice in Society,* by Richard Quinney (Boston: Little, Brown, and Co., 1969), p. 332.
17. Skolnick, "Social Control," p. 53.
18. Quoted in ibid., p. 60.
19. Blumberg, *Criminal Justice,* pp. 65–66.
20. Sudnow, "Normal Crimes," pp. 319–320.
21. Blumberg, *Criminal Justice,* p. 270.
22. Sudnow, "Normal Crimes," pp. 319–320.
23. See generally Karl Marx and Friedrich Engels, *Manifesto of the Communist Party* (Chicago: Kerr, 1906); Robert K. Merton, "Manifest and Latent Functions," in his *Social Theory and Social Structure,* rev. ed. (Glencoe, Illinois: The Free Press, 1957).

24. See for examples Issac Balbus, *The Dialects of Legal Repression: Black Rebels Before the American Courts* (New York: Russel Sage Foundation, 1972); Otto Kirchheimer, *Politics, Law, and Social Change* (New York: Columbia University Press, 1969); Otto Kirchheimer, *Political Justice: The Use of Procedure for Political Ends* (New Jersey: Princeton University Press, 1961). And see more generally Andre Gorz, "Technical Intelligence and the Capitalist Division of Labor," *Telos,* XII (Summer 1972), pp. 27–41; Serg Mallet, *La Nouvelle Classe Ouvriere* (Paris, 1963); and Ralph Miliban, *The State in Capitalist Society* (New York: Basic Books, 1969).

25. Gary Ebbels, "Las Vegas Attorney Fights for 'Defender' Association," *Las Vegas Review,* January 17, 1977, second front page.

26. Loc. cit.

27. Robert Lefort, "Lawyers for the Poor Can't Win," *Law Against the People* ed. by Robert Lefort (New York: Vintage Books, 1971), p. 130.

28. Ibid., p. 127.

29. John Conyers, Jr., "Crime-Fighting Establishment in Near Ruin," *Las Vegas Review,* January 10, 1977, p. 3.

30. Platt and Pollock, "Channeling Lawyers," p. 131.

31. Jackie Ghormley, "Legislative May Grant the Death Wish to Lifers," *Las Vegas Review,* January 20, 1977, front page.

32. Loc. cit.

33. James Q. Wilson, "Crime and the Criminologist," *The Aldine Crime and Justice Annual* (Chicago: Aldine, 1974), p. 461.

34. Seymour Halleck, "Introduction," *The Aldine Crime and Justice Annual* (Chicago: Aldine, 1974), p. xi.

35. Loc. cit.

36. Richard Quinney and John Wildeman, *The Problem of Crime: A Critical Introduction to Criminology,* 2nd ed. (New York: Harper and Row, 1977), pp. 171–172.

37. Mark C. Kennedy, "Beyond Incrimination," in *The Criminologist: Crime and the Criminal,* by Charles E. Reasons (Pacific Palisades: Goodyear, 1974), p. 295.

38. C. Wright Mills, *The Sociological Imagination* (New York: Grove Press, 1959).

39. A. C. Gumann, "Law Enforcement: A Look Into the Future," in *The Ambivalent Force: Perspective on the Police,* by A. Niederhoffer and A. Blumberg, revised ed. (New York: Rinehart, 1976), p. 131.

40. See for example Barry Krisberg, *Crime and Privilege: Towarda New Criminology* (New Jersey: Prentice-Hall, 1975), p. 143.

41. Herman and Julia Schwendinger, "Defenders of Order or Guardians of Human Rights?" *Issues in Criminology,* V, Summer 1970.

42. Platt and Pollock, "Channeling Lawyers."

43. Gregg Barak, "Community-Based Alternatives: A Change in Rehabilitation in the Developing Social and Industrial Complex?" A paper presented at the annual meeting of the American Society of Criminology, Tucson, Arizona, Nov. 6, 1976, p. 14.

Index